The British Raj

A Captivating Guide to the British in India, Starting from the Indian Rebellion of 1857 to the Indian Independence Act of 1947

Free Bonus from Captivating History (Available for a Limited time)

Hi History Lovers!

Now you have a chance to join our exclusive history list so you can get your first history ebook for free as well as discounts and a potential to get more history books for free! Simply visit the link below to join.

Captivatinghistory.com/ebook

Also, make sure to follow us on Facebook, Twitter and Youtube by searching for Captivating History.

Contents

Introduction

The British presence in India lasted for nearly 350 years, but only the last 90 were under the direct rule of the British government. To some, ninety years might seem a short period to write a history book about. However, the time of the British Raj was very influential. It brought change to Indian politics, education, society, infrastructure, industry, and other aspects of Indian life. But while the British Empire brought modernization to its colonies, that modernization came with a price.

The British Raj did not cover just where India is today. In fact, it spanned across the territories of four separate states that exist today: Bangladesh, Pakistan, India, and Burma. It is estimated that around a quarter of a million British were buried in these territories since the East India Company set its first foothold. The oldest European graves can be found in port cities such as Madras or Bombay, where the first merchants settled trading offices.

The British spread across the whole subcontinent, starting as simple merchants who wanted a piece of the riches brought by trade monopolies in the East Indies. Driving off their competitors, the Portuguese and French, the British became conquerors, submitting all of India to their will. And when the political climate changed back in Britain, India was simply transferred to the Crown, as if it was a property that could be given away.

What the British government did, albeit unknowingly, is unite all the people of the subcontinent under one nation. Before the British Raj, the demographics of India were very diverse, with people grouped in smaller nations divided by different beliefs and cultures. But with the coming of the British, the need for unity grew and finally culminated in the late 19th century with the founding of the political party known as the Indian National Congress. Finally, the struggle for the independence of the subcontinent could begin.

One person rose as a star of the independence movement, and he became the symbol of the fight against oppression all over the world: Mahatma Gandhi. He inspired people such as Martin Luther King Jr. and Nelson Mandela. His philosophy of nonviolent resistance continues to be used even today whenever the common people of the world feel the need to voice their dissatisfaction with their governments. Mahatma Gandhi wasn't alone in his fight against the British. Various individuals, both Indians and foreigners, showed up to support the independence movement and drive off the British. Each had their own reasons, but they all had the same goal, even if it meant dividing India along the religious borders of Hinduism and Islam.

Chapter 1 – East India Company, the First British Presence on the Indian Subcontinent

The coat of arms of the East India Company

https://en.wikipedia.org/wiki/East_India_Company#/media/File:Coat_of_arms _of_the_East_India_Company.svg

The East India Company was founded by a group of merchants and politicians with the goal of sailing to the East Indies and establishing a foothold on trade. The desire of these merchants to travel and trade in these distant lands was no coincidence. The growing power of Spain and Portugal in the Indian Ocean was evident as the countries were growing richer. It was not that the British had never tried to set sail to the East before, but all of their efforts had failed due to the unpredictable climate of the unknown territories.

However, their luck changed in 1592 when the English captured a Portuguese ship that carried riches obtained from India. Among them were jewels, pearls, spices, and textiles. But one of the greatest treasures the captured ship carried was a manuscript with precisely drawn and described routes used by Portuguese merchants to reach Japan, India, and China. England finally had the means to safely reach these countries and challenge the Portuguese monopoly on trade in the East Indies.

Almost a century earlier, a Portuguese explorer named Vasco da Gama discovered a safe passage to the Indies via the Cape of Good Hope in Africa. Before that, the only known route was across the land, traversing Europe and West Asia. And even though the maritime route was dangerous since tropical storms were a frequent occurrence in Asia, it was still a much faster route, which enabled the quick transport of trade goods.

The idea of the East India Company was born much earlier among the merchant-explorers who were visionary enough to expand their area of business and profit to the distant lands. However, they had no means of financing such long and dangerous trips by themselves. They needed help and the inauguration of the Company by Queen Elizabeth I. By 1599, the Company gathered more than 200 merchants, artists, and explorers willing to commit to the trade in the East Indies. A petition was sent to the queen, but the cause was blocked by Parliament, who saw the Company as a potential cause of renewed conflict with Spain and Portugal. However, in 1600, Queen

Elizabeth I issued a charter in which she gave legitimacy to the Company, naming it "The Company of the Merchants of London Trading to the East Indies."

The first East India voyage happened in 1601 with the ship named the *Red Dragon*, which was commanded by Sir James Lancaster. The Company was successful in opening two free-trade zones, then known as "factories," one in Java, and another one in the Moluccas. The *Red Dragon* returned to England in 1603, and upon its arrival, the crew learned about the end of the war with Spain and the death of Queen Elizabeth I. Because the Company was successful in breaching the Portuguese monopoly in trade, Commander Lancaster was knighted by King James I, who recognized the value of new horizons that were opened to British trade.

The Foothold in India and the Expansion

It was during the rule of Mughal Emperor Jahangir (r. 1605–1627) that the Company first came to Bengal for trade. But the Mughals were not impressed by their intentions. The British had to endure a series of defeats at the hands of the Mughals before they were able to open their "factories" in India. Not only did the Mughals oppose the British trade in India, but the British Crown was also against the Company setting a foothold in the hostile Mughal Empire. Instead, King James sent a diplomatic mission to Jahangir with the task of negotiating and arranging a trade treaty.

The mission took four years to complete, and its success completely depended on the mood of the Mughal emperor and his fondness of the British diplomats. It was of no help that the Dutch already had a foothold in the empire and did their best to frustrate the efforts of British diplomacy. It was only when the British promised to bring goods from the European market directly to the emperor that progress was made. Jahangir was pleased with the terms, and in 1620, the first British factory was opened in Surat. Immediately, the British wanted to expand their influence across the Indian subcontinent, but the unexpected high prices of traveling over the land stopped them.

A second factory was opened shortly after in Agra, but the spread of British influence was thwarted by the Portuguese presence in India. To achieve a monopoly on the trade in the East Indies, England had to conquer the Portuguese footholds on the subcontinent. The English and Portuguese were already in a conflict in Persia, where they fought over another trade monopoly, so the conquest of Bombay, Calcutta, and Madras in India is often seen as an extension of that conflict.

Madras was founded by the Company on the site of a fishing village called Madraspatnam, which was previously under Portuguese rule. This was where the British chose to build the Fort of St George in 1639 to defend British possessions from neighboring Portuguese settlements. The fort managed to attract local artisans, and it became a commercial success in just a few months.

Bombay fell in 1626 without much resistance, and the Portuguese retreated to Goa, but not for long. The Portuguese took it back shortly after, but because of the political marriage between the new British King Charles II and Portuguese Princess Catherine of Braganza, it became a part of her dowry. Seven years later, in 1668, the king gifted Bombay to the Company.

However, the history of Calcutta is far more complicated. In 1685, the East India Company requested permission to build a fortress on the banks of the Hooghly River that would protect their trade interests. Mughal Emperor Aurangzeb declined this request since he didn't want foreign fortresses built in his empire as they would represent a potential threat to him. However, the Company was determined to establish its authority in Bengal, and they used an army against the Mughals to prove their point.

The port at Chittagong was the first to fall, and the British established their currency there. The port city of Chittagong became the first city to be the property of the East India Company. The British Army was supposed to move to Dhaka next, but the winds took them by mistake to Hooghly. There, the British soldiers molested the locals, which offended the Mughal leaders, who ordered the immediate closing of all the Company's factories in Bengal. The British realized then that they would never assert their authority in Bengal unless they built a fortress. But the Mughals still wouldn't allow it, and war became the only outcome. It would either end the Company's presence in Bengal, or it would result in some kind of permission for the British to build their needed fortress. The Company lost the war, and by 1690, they were expelled from Bengal. To retaliate, the Company settled in Madras and halted all of the Mughal ships that carried Muslim pilgrims to Mecca. Emperor Aurangzeb was enraged, and another conflict arose. This time, the British won, and they forced the Mughal emperor to admit them back in Bengal.

However, the Company was still denied its fortress. The British decided to ignore the prohibition and started building what was to be known as Fort William in Calcutta. It should be noted that Calcutta wasn't a city yet. Nobody knows what was previously occupying the area. The three nearby villages of Sutanuti, Kalikata, and Gobindapur were of no importance, and they were sold to the British. In their place, Calcutta was founded.

Back at home in England, the Company had to fight Parliament, which wasn't willing to allow the Company complete autonomy as the Crown would lose profits. The East India Company got its license renewed under the same status in 1712, and by then, 15 percent of the imports in England were brought from India by the Company. It was this income from India that ensured Britain would be the birthplace of the Industrial Revolution. The Seven Years' War (1756-1763), which was originally fought between Britain and France over the colonies of North America, increased the demand for Indian goods and raw materials that were used to sustain the army. Britain was in dire need of an efficient method of production, and thus, it became the leader in industrialization. As a result, the standard of living increased throughout the country. The demand for luxury goods from India only continued to increase as the demand back home grew. Soon, the East India Company became the single largest trade institution in the British global market.

The Seven Years' War wasn't only fought in the territories of North America. It also extended to the Indian subcontinent, as the French East India Company had an interest in the trade in the East. Britain was victorious on all fronts, which resulted in France limiting its ambitions for trade. The Industrial Revolution in France was halted by this defeat, as some of the Indian territories that were under their control were lost. Britain gained Pondicherry, Mahe, Karaikal, and Chandernagar. However, France was still present in India with a military force, which presented itself as a constant threat to the British East India Company, especially during the American Revolution, as British soldiers were often recalled to fight on another front.

It was the French Revolutionary Wars (1792–1802) that secured even more losses of French territories in India. Although France would remain present in the Indian subcontinent for the next 200 years, the trade interest of this European state would continue to steadily decline. The British East India Company virtually had no economic competition, but it would face revolts by the locals.

Modernization of India

In 1796, the British East India Company's governor-general started the reorganization of the Company's army. The Company had paid the native soldiers it employed well and gave them training in the European style of warfare ever since they were first introduced to the army. They were acquainted with modern weapons and the red coats of the British soldiers, and they were well-disciplined soldiers who willingly chose to fight for the Company because the pay was well beyond what the local rulers would pay and because it was regular work. Being a sepoy, which is what Indian soldiers serving under the British were called, was very popular, and the Company was able to afford a very large army. By 1806, the sepoys of the East India Company numbered 154,500, which made them one of the largest armies in the world. As the Company gained new territories, they needed to employ the local police. The police weren't as well trained as the army, but they were effective in dealing with issues regarding the Company on a local level. During the years, as even more territory was conquered, the Company had to transform the local police to local regiments. Garrisons were built, and depending on the location and need, it was filled with infantry or cavalry, sometimes even both. As the political picture on the Indian subcontinent changed, many armies of the local rulers joined the Company, obliged either by treaties, diplomatic efforts, or simply by conquest.

At first, the policy of the Company was to adjust the British people who served in India to the "Oriental" way of life. This means that the British generals and officers who served in India (most of them doing so their whole lives) had to learn the language and, for the most part, get used to the cultural differences between their European lives and the Indians. However, by 1813, the Company's politics had changed due to the influence of evangelical teachings back home.

At this point, the Company strived to use their Christian and Utilitarian philosophy to anglicize and modernize the people of India. The Christian missionaries started increasing their activity on the Indian subcontinent. The governor-general banned the Indian custom of *sati*, in which widows were burned alive on top of their husband's funeral pyre. The other changes the Company implemented also elevated the status of women in Indian society. The Company also strived to open schools for Indian children, which would teach them everything in the English language exclusively. However, the Company lacked the money for social projects and modernization on such a large scale.

Aside from banning *sati*, the Company's rule tried to help the position of women by rewarding people who married widows. However, for the conservative society of India, it wasn't enough for the British rulers to bring new laws to their country. They would often be disobeyed simply because they clashed with Indian customs and traditions. Even those who agreed to marry widows would soon abandon them. The men of India thought that nothing good could come out of a marriage with another man's wife, even if he was deceased. The Company's effort of reintroducing widows to society was mostly criticized by Brahmins, the highest caste in India and whose support the British relied on the most. The widows who were not burned after their husband's death were essentially condemned by the society in which they grew up. They were forced to step into the service of the British as housemaids, servants, or even lovers if they were still young and beautiful.

When it comes to the modernization of India, the Company invested only in those segments of life that would serve to increase its profits. The postal service was introduced to India in 1837, but it only connected the cities that were under the rule of the Company. Later, the postal service was expanded to the regions where the Company had its representatives, even if the Company had no direct control there. But the post offices it would open served all of the public, and any citizen could benefit from them. Although the Indian subcontinent had developed the courier service, the use of it was strictly limited to rulers and noblemen of higher classes.

By the mid-19th century, electricity was introduced to India, and with it, the Company brought telegraphy. However, in the beginning, telegraph services were only used for shipping-related businesses. Four telegraph offices were built along the Hooghly River to connect the line between Calcutta and Diamond Harbour. By 1855, the governor-general of India, Lord Dalhousie, was permitted to build 41 more offices and a line that would connect Calcutta to Agra, Agra to Bombay, Agra to Peshawar, and Bombay to Madras. This line would be expanded by 1857 to 62 offices. Telegraph services became public in 1855 and were available to everyone.

The railway was one of the services the Company needed the most, as trains would ship trade goods much faster from the production lines to the ports. However, even though the railway network connected the Isle of Britain by 1845, India posed a challenge with its uncommon and very diverse climate, monsoon seasons, lush vegetation, floods, and tropical storms in coastal areas. In 1849, it was decided to build three railways, which the British would observe and then decide if it was profitable enough to invest in connecting the whole Indian subcontinent. The first railway line to be completed was a 21-mile stretch that connected Bombay and Thane. It was completed in 1853, and from there, the railway network across India continued to grow. But railway construction was still very new, and India had no experts capable of building a large-scale system that would connect the whole subcontinent, so the engineers from England had to be brought in. This increased the price and time of the construction since the British experts had to get introduced to the land itself. By the end of the Company's rule in India, the railway network was only at its birth. But what the Company did was set the foundation for India to continue to build railways and go forward in the modernization of the subcontinent.

The First Conflicts

Robert Clive and Emperor Shah Allam

During the expansion of its influence, the East India Company experienced constant resistance from the local rulers. The Battle of Plassey in 1757 is considered the beginning of British rule in India, as it was the first armed conflict against a local ruler, the nawab of Bengal, Siraj-ud-Daulah. He was allied with the French, with whom England had already fought the Seven Years' War. The Battle of Plassey is often seen as an extension of the Seven Years' War; however, it should be noted that the Company fought for its interests, not just for the Kingdom of Great Britain. France wanted a monopoly on trade in the East Indies too, and the French East India Company already had a foothold on the subcontinent and wanted to keep the British out. The British victory over the Nawab of Bengal and his French allies ensured that the trade monopoly belonged to the British East India Company. With Bengal firmly under its control, the British East India Company seized control of the entire Indian subcontinent over the next 100 years.

The British victory at the Battle of Plassey led to an estrangement between the Company and the Mughal Empire, as the nawab of Bengal, Siraj-ud-Daulah, was a Mughal ally. The cold relations between the empire and the Company led to the Battle of Buxar, which took place on October 22nd, 1764. The conflict was resolved by the Treaty of Allahabad, which was signed between Emperor Shah Alam II (r. 1760–1788 and 1788–1806) and Robert Clive of the East India Company and the first British governor of Bengal. This treaty marked the period of British political and constitutional rule of India, as the Mughal Empire gave the Company the right to collect the revenues throughout the empire. In return, the Company paid Shah Alam a yearly tribute, which the emperor used to maintain his royal court. Thus, the Mughal dominance of India came to an end.

Between 1775 and 1818, the British East India Company was at war with the Maratha Confederacy on three separate occasions. Maratha was an empire that was formed in the 17th century by the Marathi-speaking warrior people from the west of the Deccan Plateau.

They were the ones who liberated most of the Indian subcontinent from the Mughal Empire. The First Anglo-Maratha War, which lasted from 1775 to 1782, was fought because the Company decided to meddle in the dynastic struggle of the empire. The Company won, and the outcome was the spread of the Company's influence over the territories of the Maratha Empire. Besides this, the Marathas were to prohibit the French East India Company from gaining a foothold in their territories, securing the monopoly of the British Company on trade in the East Indies.

The Second Anglo-Maratha War, which took place between 1803 and 1805, was fought due to the internal struggles in the Maratha Empire. At the time, the empire was a confederation led by five warlords who constantly engaged in internal conflicts. To protect its interests, the Company gave its support to Baji Rao II, the peshwa of the empire (somewhat similar to a prime minister), who agreed on a treaty that would doom the Maratha territories to submit to British rule. Not all of the warlords accepted the treaty, which led to the Second Anglo-Maratha War. All of the warlords eventually submitted, and the Maratha Empire became a client state to the British East India Company.

The Third Anglo-Maratha War, which lasted from 1817 to 1818, started because of a rebellion led by Peshwa Baji Rao II. Although he had allied with the British in the previous war, he was now unsatisfied with the Company's ever-growing power and the decline of his empire. However, the Company proved to be victorious, even though its army was significantly outnumbered. The Company had modern military technology and training, though, while the Marathas were stubborn in using their old ways of warfare. It was after the Third Anglo-Maratha War that the British East India Company gained control over the whole subcontinent. The Maratha Empire lost its independence, and it simply collapsed. Some of its territories were annexed and formed the Central Provinces of British India.

For the next three decades, the East India Company had full control over the entirety of India, and they profited greatly. They even took the opportunity to confiscate some of the colonies that had belonged to other European nations, such as the Islands of Réunion and Mauritius, which were French possessions. The Dutch Maluku Islands, better known as the Spice Islands, fell into British hands after the invasion. With them, the Company gained the riches that came with the production and trade in spices such as nutmeg and cloves. When Java fell to the British, the Dutch lost their foothold in the East Indies altogether.

Back home in the British Isles, the Protestant revival movement was growing. The Company was influenced by the movement, and it organized a systematic spreading of the religion throughout its colonies. Although the Company officially recognized and respected Hinduism and Islam in India, its members were very disrespectful of the social constructs, castes, and ethnic groups that belonged to them. It was the growth of tensions between the East India Company and the local religious and cultural groups, which would eventually spark a mutiny in 1824 and 1857.

The Barrackpore Mutiny

It was during the First Anglo-Burmese War that the order for a march of nearly 500 miles (800 kilometers) was sent to three regiments of the Bengal Native Infantry. They were to traverse the distance between Calcutta in Bengal to Chittagong (in today's Bangladesh), where they would be stationed in preparation for the front in Burma. However, this march presented several problems to the sepoys. Initially, the Burmese were victorious against the British, which led Indians to believe that their enemy had supernatural powers. As such, they were reluctant to fight against the Burmese. On top of that, these regiments had just finished a very long march from Mathura to Barrackpore, and they were tired and in need of rest and resupply.

But the alternative to the march to Chittagong was even worse to the sepoys. The sepoys were mostly recruited from the higher castes of Indians, and to them, crossing the water was a taboo. Taking a ship to their destination was sacrilege to them, and the British East India Company had to comply with their religious beliefs. This taboo is known as kala pani ("black water"), and Hindu people believed that if they crossed the waters to reach foreign lands, they would lose social respect and their cultural character. The only viable way to transport sepoys from one part of the country to another was by land. However, the railway network didn't reach all the parts of the subcontinent yet, and the sepoys had no choice but to march.

Another taboo among high-caste Indians required them to prepare their food and eat it from separate cooking utensils, which were usually made out of heavy brass. This meant that every soldier had his own heavy pack to carry during the march, making it even harder on them. Besides the pack, which contained food, utensils, blankets, and ammo, the sepoys were required to carry their muskets.

The sepoys demanded that the Company provide them with either bulls to pull their equipment and lessen the weight from the soldiers' backs or be paid extra money so they could buy the animals themselves. However, the Company declined the request of its soldiers, offering them the advice of discarding anything that was not necessary from their backpacks. The sepoys insisted on their demands because they could not break their own religious beliefs. That is when the Company chose to threaten the sepoys, declaring that if they did not stop complaining, they would be shipped to Chittagong by sea.

The sepoys wrote a petition to the commander-in-chief of India, Edward Paget, and patiently waited for the reply. When Paget heard about the situation in Barrackpore, he decided to personally deal with the matter and moved there from Calcutta. Paget was very conservative in his military ways, and the complaints of the sepoys sounded to him as a preparation for mutiny. He brought with him the

European troops from Calcutta and ordered them to attack the disobeying regiments of the Bengal Native Infantry.

Depiction of General Edward Paget

https://upload.wikimedia.org/wikipedia/commons/d/d1/
Sir_Edward_Paget_by_Martin_Archer_Shee_1810.jpg

The final order for the rebels to lay down their weapons was sent on November 2nd, 1824, but the commander-in-chief anticipated the refusal and had already organized the attack. The loyal army was sent to surround the encampment of the sepoys and wait for further orders. Paget ordered fire on the sepoys when he didn't receive any reply. In a panic, the sepoys tried to flee, but all the exits from the camp were blocked. The Europeans and Indian loyalists engaged in what can only be described as a massacre. Many bystanders, local people, women, and children were slaughtered during the operation. After the attack was over, an investigation concluded that the rebels had no violent intentions as they hadn't even bothered to load their muskets.

The leader of the rebelling sepoys was quickly tried and hanged. Those who didn't die during the massacre were arrested and then sentenced to many years of hard labor. Eleven more sepoys were singled out as probable leaders, and they were all convicted to death by hanging. The 47th Regiment of the Bengal Native Infantry was disbanded, and the Indian officers were all disgraced and weren't even seen as worthy enough to serve the government. All of the British officers who were in charge of the sepoy regiments, even though they could not deal with the mutiny, were moved to other regiments, where they continued their service as if nothing had happened.

It is generally believed that the sepoy protest was a peaceful one and that the British government of India used violence to suppress it. To preserve the image of the Company, no news agencies were allowed to report on the mutiny in Barrackpore in either Calcutta or London. The official statement was printed in the *Calcutta Gazette*, but it mentioned the rebellion as a trivial little uprising that was dealt with swiftly and without any casualties. The first criticism of the events happened six months later, in the *Oriental Herald*, which accused the British officers of slaughtering the sepoys. When other sepoys finally learned the truth about the incident, many deserted the British Army. The general atmosphere of distrust between the Indian soldiers and their British officers was created, and it would eventually lead to the great rebellion of 1857 and the disassembly of the East India Company.

Chapter 2 – The Rebellion of 1857 and the Fall of the Company

A scene from the 1857 rebellion

https://en.wikipedia.org/wiki/File:Sepoy_Mutiny_1857.png

Prelude

For over thirty years, ever since the mutiny of 1824, the sepoys remained concerned about their religious rights during their servitude in the Bengal Native Infantry. The East India Company did nothing to persuade its Hindu and Muslim soldiers that their culture and religion would be respected. The Company continued the practice of recruiting from high-caste Indians and wealthy Muslim families, and both of these groups had their own concerns about their status in the army. Hindus still believed in kala pani, and they preferred to march instead of sail. But in 1856, the Company issued an act in which all new recruits were obliged to travel on the seas. Although the act didn't involve the sepoys who were already serving, they raised concerns about applying the act in the future. Their worries were amplified by the fact that the numbers of Christian evangelists in India kept rising. Soon, the rumor started that the Company was preparing to convert all Indians to Christianity.

The final drop for the sepoys was the introduction of new ammunition for the muskets. The ammo was packed in paper cartridges, which needed to be bitten off before it was used. In general, this wouldn't be a problem as long as the paper wasn't greased with what the sepoys presumed to be cow and pig tallow. For Hindus and Muslims, consuming these animals was strictly prohibited. Even putting the cartridges near their mouths was sacrilege for the religious sepoys. Soon, they started protesting, and it didn't matter that the Company promised the grease on the paper wasn't animal fat. The distrust toward the British officers was too great by this point, and when the Company announced a new model of cartridges that could be torn off, not bitten, the sepoys only believed that their previous fears were now justified.

As if it was some kind of curse, the birthplace of the rebellion that would bring down the Company happened to be the same place where the previous rebellion of 1824 happened. A sepoy named Mangal Pandey was angered by the disrespect shown to his religion and culture and wanted to do something about it. Many eyewitnesses claimed that Mangal Pandey was in some kind of religious trance when he fired at his sergeant major, who only wanted to calm Pandey down. The incident happened on March 29th, 1857, and the order to arrest Pandey was issued immediately, but no Indian sepoy would come near him. Seeing how he failed to inspire his comrades to mutiny, Mangal Pandey shot himself. But he only managed to wound himself, and he was arrested since he was now unable to put up a resistance.

As if it was a collective mutiny, the whole 34th Regiment, to which Pandey belonged, was dismissed and dishonored. Mangal Pandey was hanged for his actions on April 8th, 1857. The soldier who dared to arrest Mangal was promoted, but he didn't get to enjoy his new rank of sergeant as he was killed only six weeks after the death of Pandey. The culprits were the ex-members of the 34th Regiment of the Bengal Native Infantry.

Although Pandey didn't live to see the uprising, the story of his actions quickly spread through other regiments of the army. His death was the opening act of what would become the Indian Rebellion of 1857. He became not just the role model of the later rebel leaders, but he was also lifted to the position of a national hero. The modern Indian nationalist party often portrays Mangal Pandey as a mastermind who sacrificed himself to start the revolt against the East India Company, even though he claimed during the trial that he was under the influence of opium and couldn't even remember his actions.

Soon, the unrest started spreading. In April, Agra, Allahabad, and Ambala were burning. The sepoys did not openly rebel yet, but they were resorting to arson in protest over the cartridges and the general treatment of their cultures and religions. On April 24th, in Meerut, one of the biggest unrests occurred. The sepoys there refused to use the new cartridges during the firing drill, and as a punishment, they were all arrested. Eighty-five Indian soldiers were sentenced to ten years of imprisonment and hard labor. But the actions of the British officers were what caused the unrest the next day. They chose to publicly strip the sepoys of their uniforms to humiliate them in front of other regiments. Instead of provoking fear in the remaining soldiers, the British only managed to instigate their anger.

Meerut was also home to a very large British force, which had over 2,000 British soldiers serving there. The next day, it was the British soldiers who suffered, as the remaining sepoys demanded revenge. The Indian soldiers planned to release their comrades by any means necessary, and the revolt was led by the 3rd Cavalry. It was the European junior officers that were killed first, as they tried to stop the mutiny early. The superior officers were warned about the possible revolt, but they decided to do nothing as it was Sunday, a day for rest and reflection. Civilian quarters were also attacked, and a few women and children were killed. Off-duty soldiers who found themselves in the city bazaar were attacked by angry mobs, as the revolt began to be supported by the Indian civilians who supported sepoys. Some servants and Indian civilians helped the British officers by moving them out of the streets, but once they made sure the Europeans were safe, they joined the protesters on the streets of Meerut. Some sepoys showed similar care for the trusted British officers, women, and children, who were escorted to safety during the mutiny.

Rebelling sepoys moved from Meerut to Delhi, which was only forty miles away. There, on May 11th, they appealed to Bahadur Shah (1837–1857), the last Mughal emperor, to lead them. However, Bahadur Shah was an emperor in name only, as his rule was limited just to the city of Delhi. He was a puppet emperor who served the East India Company, and for it, he received a pension to maintain his status and court. He was content with his position as a puppet emperor, and he ignored the sepoys who called on him. However, Bahadur Shah's court abandoned him and joined the revolt, thus forcing the old emperor to acknowledge the rebellion.

Delhi had a large depot of ammunition and weapons, and fearing that the rebelling sepoys would get their hands on it, the British officers ordered an attack. In a panic, they killed their own guards who were stationed to protect the arsenal of Delhi. The sepoys were too many, though, and they kept coming at the British soldiers. Seeing that it was impossible to protect the arsenal from the rebels, the British decided to blow it up. The blast was massive, killing many civilians on the streets. This massive explosion and killing of civilians angered the rest of the sepoys, who had been reluctant to join the rebellion. The ranks of the rebels started swelling even more as a result.

Many Europeans fled the city in their carriages or on foot. Some were helped by loyal Indian servants or villagers, but many were killed trying to reach Meerut. Most of the Europeans in Delhi were civilians, merchants, and engineers of the British Empire, and they had been living in India together with their wives and children. Unfortunately, they were in the middle of the conflict and became one of the first victims. As if that wasn't enough, Bahadur Shah ordered all Europeans who were imprisoned during the unrest and those found hiding in Delhi to be executed in the courtyard of the palace.

Once Delhi fell, the reaction of the British officers led to many more sepoys joining the rebellion. A small number of Brits trusted the sepoys that they commanded, but many more tried to contain and disarm their soldiers to prevent the mutiny from spreading. This only instigated sepoys into open rebellion against their commanders. The military and civilian administrators were quick to remove themselves from the cities and take their families to safety. This was seen as abandonment by many loyal Indian soldiers, who then decided to join the rebellion. However, Muslim soldiers were not sure how to react. They didn't have the same resentment for their British officers as the Hindus, and the Islamic religious leaders couldn't agree on whether to proclaim jihad or not. Although some Muslim soldiers took up arms against the British, a large number of them remained loyal to the Company and offered their support against the sepoys.

The Revolt

The Mughal rulers lost their power over the northern parts of the Indian subcontinent once the British East India Company conquered their lands. However, their name still resonated strongly among the Indian people, both commoners and nobility. The Mughals even evoked the feeling of respect among foreign leaders. As the sepoys had no Indian officers to lead them, the natural choice was their old emperor, who enjoyed his pension paid by the Company. Some historians believe that Bahadur Shah was stubborn and didn't want to join the rebellion until he was openly threatened by his people and the nobility of his court. The first thing Bahadur Shah did once he was officially proclaimed the emperor of India was to issue his own coinage to assert his new power. However, this proclamation of the Mughal emperor as an Indian leader turned the Sikhs and the state of Punjab away from rebellion, and they offered their support to the British to avoid returning to Islamic rule.

During the first conflicts with the British, the Indian forces were able to push forward and take some of the strategically important towns in the provinces of Haryana and Bihar, as well as the Central and United Provinces of Agra and Awadh. However, the sepoy mutineers lacked a centralized command, as their emperor was that only in name. Bahadur Shah was too old (he was in his eighties), and his sons, the princes, and nobility lacked the knowledge of warfare. Some of the sepoys showed a natural predisposition for leadership, and later, the emperor officially proclaimed them commanders-in-chief. One such man was Bakht Khan, who replaced the emperor's son, Mirza Mughal, when he proved to be an inefficient leader

The sepoys weren't the only ones who resented the British rule in India. The agricultural societies of some provinces rose into a civil rebellion because of the unjust treatment by the British. Because of the uprising of the Indian soldiers, the civilians felt brave enough to start opposing the British administration, which had given the Company unlimited rights over the land, leaving the peasants in perpetual poverty. The civilian revolutionaries were large in number, and that number only multiplied once they opened the British prisons and released all the Indian people who had been condemned by the British. Even though the revolt started as a military mutiny, it grew to become an uprising of the general populace.

The rebels felt the need for some kind of institutional entity that would provide them legitimacy and secure the territories that had been newly taken from the British. The emperor was just a symbol after all and was not at all capable of leading the state. A council was formed to deal with all the legislative and administrative matters, but the Company organized its counterattack soon enough, and it stopped all the efforts of the rebels to further organize and build a new state.

It didn't help that the rebels couldn't agree on their plans for the future. They did not share the same political perspective, and because of the many disagreements that arose, they were unable to bring to life a new political order. The Company even admitted later that India would have been lost to Britain if only one able leader had risen from the ranks of the rebels. The rebels were united only by their common hatred for the British rule, and this hatred wasn't enough. Each group of rebels fought for their own reasons, and the communication between the leaders was almost nonexistent. In some areas, the rebels were completely unaware of the fights won and lost in the neighboring provinces. But they did show remarkable courage, dedication, and commitment, and they managed to bring the Company to its knees.

The Siege of Delhi

Depiction of the siege of Delhi

https://upload.wikimedia.org/wikipedia/commons/4/47/
Capture_of_Delhi%2C_1857.jpg

Having their military ranks significantly reduced (it is estimated that half of the total number of the Company's army joined the rebellion), the British sent for help. Due to the loss of loyal sepoys, they were very slow at organizing their counterattack. They waited for the British troops to arrive from either home or other colonies, which took months. Some soldiers were sent by sea, while others had to cross Persia because they had been fighting the Crimean War with the Russians (1853–1856). It took the Company two months to organize their field forces and start a counterattack. Two columns from Meerut and Shimla were sent on a march to Delhi. On their way, they killed many Indians, disregarding whether they belonged to the rebels or not. The British forces met at Karnal, and joined by contractors from the Kingdom of Nepal, they fought the main rebel army at the Battle of Badli-ki-Serai on June 8th, 1857.

The numbers of the rebel army remain a mystery. In some contemporary works, the strength of the rebels was estimated to be 30,000; however, modern historians believe this number to be an exaggeration. The realistic numbers are somewhere between 4,000 and 9,000. However, the rebels didn't have many firearms, as they relied on what they could capture from the British. Their numbers were largely bolstered by the civilians, who fought with swords, hooks, and pitchforks.

Although the British Army was greatly outnumbered by the sepoys and the civilians who joined them, the tactics they used brought them victory. The British were able to capture the gun stations in the villages surrounding Delhi, as the scared sepoys retreated. They ran to Delhi, bringing the news of the British Army being on its way. This news scared most of the civilians, who then abandoned the rebellion. But the British Army was tired, as the newly arrived soldiers from Britain and Crimea weren't accustomed to the climate of the Indian subcontinent. They suffered from both exhaustion and diseases, and they were in no condition to attack Delhi. Instead, they opted to lay siege.

Even when the British were finally ready to order the attack, the disorganization of the communication network led to confusion. The order demanded an attack on the city by the morning of July 14th, but it didn't reach all the officers in time. The attack had to be called off, and the siege continued. This confusion gave the rebels much-needed time, as their reinforcement from other provinces had finally arrived. The rebels from within the city attacked the British soldiers on two separate occasions and were very close to driving them off. However, the rebels continued to retreat at crucial points of the battle, achieving little.

In the meantime, the British ranks were decimated as cholera spread throughout their ranks. Even the officers succumbed to this disease and had to be replaced by less competent soldiers of lower ranks. Archdale Wilson was promoted to the rank of general due to this, but he did nothing to improve the conditions for his soldiers. It was the perfect time for the rebels to strike, but they had troubles of their own. Previous failures had demoralized the sepoys, and they refused to attack. The British finally received the help they needed with the arrival of the Punjab forces. With them, the British had all the needed artillery to bring Delhi down.

Brigadier General John Nicholson organized the bombardment of the city. He constructed four batteries consisting of various types of guns. Gunfire was opened strategically to fool the rebels into thinking that the main attack would come from the east. But the British attacked from the north, breaching the wall of Delhi on September 14th, 1857. Soon, the infantry and the cavalry stormed the city.

The rebels lacked the gunpowder and ammunition to efficiently fight off the attacks, and the morale of the army went even lower. They lost some parts of the city before they gathered enough courage to defend what remained. At one point, the rebels even forced the British to retreat and find shelter at the Church of Saint James. Archdale Wilson wanted to call for a retreat, but John Nicholson, who was mortally wounded, threatened that he would shoot him if such an order was given. In the end, it was decided that the British and the Company's army should hold their position and secure the parts of the city that they had gained.

Now the British Army was demoralized, and they gave in to drinking the alcohol they had looted during the attack. The rebels were not in a better position, as they lacked food. Both sides were in a rough spot and did not have the strength to organize another attack. Eventually, Wilson tried to bring discipline back among his soldiers and ordered the destruction of the confiscated alcohol. With renewed strength, the British managed to capture the city arsenal on September 16th. In two days, they cleansed the city of any rebel forces and forced Emperor Bahadur Shah to flee. The Company declared victory on September 21st, and Delhi was once again in their hands. John Nicholson died the next day.

The city was looted by the British soldiers for the next four days. Even though their official loss numbered 1,817 soldiers, it is impossible to say how many sepoys or civilians lost their lives. The rebels who were not killed during the attack were captured and imprisoned. However, the cost of victory left the Company with no means to feed both their soldiers and their prisoners. The choice was easy for the British, who wanted revenge for their fallen comrades. All of their prisoners were killed without so much as a trial.

Bahadur Shah was found six miles from Delhi. Together with his sons, he was captured and brought back to Delhi, where he was promised mercy. However, no such promise was offered to his three sons, who were all killed. Their heads were presented to the Mughal emperor, which, according to contemporary sources, depressed him so much that he refused to eat.

Campaigns in Other Provinces

In Cawnpore (Kanpur), a rebellion was led by the peshwa of the Maratha Empire, Nana Saheb (although the Maratha Empire had officially ended, the ruler kept some degree of authority). There, the Europeans were besieged in an entrenchment to the south of the city. The British major general in Cawnpore was Sir Hugh Massy Wheeler, who relied on his prestige and ability to negotiate with Nana Saheb, as he was married to a high-caste Indian woman and was a well-respected veteran. He did almost nothing to secure his people or fortify their quarters. The Europeans managed to survive the siege for three weeks before they were forced to surrender to the rebels because of the lack of food. But they demanded safe passage to Allahabad, which was granted on June 27th, 1857. Nana Saheb even provided ships that would transport them. However, while preparing to board the ships, someone from the rebel forces accidentally shot his weapon, and the frightened British started shooting, making it impossible to prevent a massacre.

The rebels killed almost everyone; only four men survived and reached Allahabad. Around 206 women and children were taken as hostages. Initially, Nana Saheb wanted the prisoners alive, but as the Company's relief army closed in on his rebel group, he ordered them all to be killed. All but five of the sepoys refused to do it, and these five men entered Bibighar ("House of the Ladies"), where the prisoners were held, and there they massacred women and children. This event is remembered as the Bibighar massacre, which took place on July 15th, 1857. Of course, the massacre only angered the British. After the massacre, the British Army used the phrase "Remember Cawnpore!" before each battle, adopting it as their official war cry. The British commander of the relief army was perhaps even more ruthless than Nana Saheb. While on the march from Allahabad to Cawnpore, two weeks before the Bibighar massacre even happened, he ordered all the villages on their way to be burned and all the peasants killed. His actions only pushed the undecided and neutral Indian citizens and sepoys to join the rebellion.

The rebels also besieged Lucknow, where around 1,700 loyal Europeans and sepoys served the British commissioner. For three months, the rebels bombarded Lucknow, trying to breach its defenses and enter the garrison, but they were unsuccessful. By the end of the siege, there were only 650 British defenders left, together with around 500 civilians. On September 25th, help was sent from Cawnpore under the leadership of Sir Henry Havelock, but his column was very small, and although they defeated the rebels, they couldn't break the siege. Instead, they were forced to join the British garrison. In October, another relief army was sent to Lucknow, who finally managed to evacuate the besieged Europeans. They decided to withdraw and not engage the rebels in an open battle, as they had a large number of women and children under their protection. They retreated to Cawnpore, and the rebels tried to retake the city. The Second Battle of Cawnpore took place on December 5th, 1857, in which the British won and thwarted the rebels' endeavors to recapture both Cawnpore and Lucknow.

In Bihar, the rebellion was mainly contained in one region, with smaller plunders and raids happening throughout the state. One of the bigger conflicts in the area started on July 25th in the Davanpur garrison. There, the sepoys of the Bengal Native Infantry planned to besiege the city of Arrah. However, the Europeans who inhabited that city were anticipating the mutiny and had not been lying idle. They chose the house of Richard Vicars Boyle, an engineer in the employment of the Company, as the safest place, and they built barricades around it. Once the rebels came, they couldn't do much but lay siege to the house that hid the Europeans of the city. When the British heard about the trapped Europeans, they sent a relief army that managed to fight off the rebels and free their comrades.

Punjab had only limited rebel activities, as the mutineer sepoys didn't have the support of the civilians. The garrisons in Punjab also didn't have well-organized communication with each other, so if the mutiny erupted in one of the compounds, others wouldn't even hear about it, let alone join them. Most of the mutineers who rose against their superiors in Punjab simply left the garrisons and marched to Delhi to join the main rebel army.

Almost all of the Indian subcontinent experienced uprisings to some degree. Some were easily dealt with, as the rebels were cut off from their main army, while others were lost because the British were forced to abandon their posts. However, it wasn't only the Indian subcontinent that rose against British rule in 1857. Other British colonies with Indian populations experienced uprisings too. These were often referred to as copycat rebellions, and they mostly happened on the islands of Southeast Asia, known as the Straits Settlements. Trinidad also saw a minor uprising, but the British secured the situation there before it could escalate. The British penal settlements of Burma and Penang demanded boosted security when the unrest spread among the imprisoned Indians. However, a quick British reaction prevented the outbreak of a rebellion.

Queen Rani of Jhansi

The area of Central India (now parts of Madhya Pradesh and Rajasthan) consisted of 6 large and almost 150 smaller states. They were under the nominal rule of the Mughal and Maratha princes, but they were all administered by the East India Company. There, the opposition to the British rule was largely centered in the Jhansi state, where Rani Lakshmibai defied the British. The Europeans sought to annex this state using a policy known as the doctrine of lapse, which stated that the area governed by a prince would be absorbed if the ruler died without a male heir. Although Rani Lakshmibai and her husband, Gangadhar Rao Newalkar, had adopted a son, the British refused to recognize the young prince as the heir of Jhansi once Gangadhar Rao died, since he wasn't their biological child.

Queen Rani in her cavalry uniform

https://en.wikipedia.org/wiki/Rani_of_Jhansi#/media/
File:Rani_of_jhansi.jpg

Rani Lakshmibai was the complete opposite of what the patriarchal society of India wanted females to be at that time. She was well educated, and besides her interests in reading and writing, she was also skillful in shooting, horsemanship, and close combat. Her childhood friends were prominent leaders of the rebellion against the British East India Company. The reason for Rani's unconventional education might be due to the loss of her mother at a young age. She was brought up among the men of the household while her father worked for the peshwa of the Bithoor district.

When the rebellion first broke out in Meerut, Rani didn't want to oppose the British rule, which had allowed her to raise an army for personal protection. However, she openly defied the British authorities when she organized a social gathering in the form of a ceremony for married women (Haldi Kumkum). The ceremony also served as an assurance to her subjects that the British were weak and that they could be easily defeated. In June of 1857, the 12th Bengal Native Infantry Regiment attacked the Star Fort of Jhansi, taking all its treasure and ammunition. Even though they promised the British soldiers that they wouldn't be hurt if they surrendered, the Indians killed them all. Although Rani claimed that she did not organize the mutiny, the British still thought she was responsible.

Only four days later, the rebels threatened Rani, and she was forced to give them enough money to secure their passage out of Jhansi. As she was still the official ruler, she did her duty and notified the British authorities of what had happened to her. Trusting her good intentions, the Company gave her the administrative power over Jhansi until the arrival of the British commander who would take up the rule.

In the meantime, one of the nephews of her deceased husband thought the opportunity had arisen to take over Jhansi, but he didn't expect Rani to be able to defend her kingdom. She gathered her private army and personally commanded the successful defense. However, it turns out the British commander wasn't actually coming. Secretly, the Company sent the armies of Orchha and Datia, their allies, to invade Jhansi and divide it between themselves. But Rani was determined to defend her kingdom once more, as she was unaware of the Company's plans to annex Jhansi.

The invaders were repelled, as Rani was a good leader and tactician. She kept Jhansi peaceful for the next six months, still waiting for the British to send their commander. As no word was coming, her advisors persuaded her to proclaim independence. The British finally arrived in March 1858, but the city was well defended and wouldn't allow them entrance. Rani was smart enough to spend her funds in opening up a foundry, which produced cannons. Her army was also bolstered by the sepoys who had abandoned their posts and wanted to join the rebellion.

The commander of the British Army, Hugh Rose, demanded the surrender of the city, threatening its destruction if his order was refused. But Rani wasn't scared, and she lifted the morale of her army with a speech in which she confirmed her intentions for Jhansi to be independent of British rule. The siege of the city started on March 23rd, 1858. The bombardment was very heavy, and even the help of Tatya Tope and his 20,000 rebels wasn't enough to beat the British. The city walls were breached on April 2nd, and once the British entered the city, the fighting on the streets began. The bravery and determination of the Indians were such that in two days, the British armies weren't able to secure even one district for themselves.

However, Rani decided that the resistance in the city was useless and that it would be wiser if she joined the forces of the main resistance of Nana Saheb and Tatya Tope. During the night, Rani escaped the city with her guards and joined the fellow resistance leaders in Kalpi. On May 22nd, the British attacked Kalpi, and Rani herself led the resistance forces. However, she was defeated and was once again forced to flee. This time, she was accompanied by the other leaders of the rebellion, and they fled to Gwalior. They joined the Indian forces there who occupied Gwalior Fort, and they proclaimed Nana Saheb to be the peshwa of the renewed, free Kingdom of Maratha. Rani was convinced that the British would follow them, and she tried to persuade her comrades to prepare the defenses of Gwalior, but they wouldn't listen. Rani was right, as Sir Hugh Rose led an attack on the city on June 16th.

Rani Lakshmibai tried to leave the area, but her way was blocked by the 8th King's Royal Irish Hussars, who killed 5,000 of her soldiers. According to eyewitnesses, Rani wore the uniform of a *sowar* (cavalryman) and engaged one of the Hussars in close combat. She was dismounted and wounded. Bleeding, she tried to kill the soldier by firing her gun at him, but she missed. The Hussar approached her and killed her with his rifle.

Tatya Tope fled to Rajputana once Gwalior was lost to the British. He was pursued by many British commanders, but he was able to raise large forces of rebels wherever he went. Even after the Revolt of 1857 was officially put down by the British, Tatya Tope continued to resist, fighting with his guerilla forces from the jungles. In the end, he, too, was captured, tried, and executed in 1859.

Once the British took Gwalior, Sir Hugh Rose wrote a report to the British command, and in it, he described Rani as one of the most beautiful and dangerous leaders of all the Indians. He also reported her burial with all the ceremonies, and he claimed he saw her bones and ashes. In India, Rani Lakshmibai is remembered as one of the greatest leaders of the rebellion. In the eyes of her nation, Rani lived and died for her country, and because of it, she was made into one of the greatest symbols of the fight against the British Raj.

The End of the Revolt

After Bahadur Shah, the last Mughal emperor, was captured, he was taken to Delhi, where he was tried. His trial lasted for over forty days, and over twenty witnesses came forward to claim that he was the main leader of the rebellion. The old emperor claimed he had no other choice as he was used by the sepoys. The 82-year-old emperor wasn't able to provide any real leadership to the rebellion, but he was tried as the primary perpetrator of the events of 1857. He was found guilty and sentenced to exile in Burma, as the Company had no power to execute an emperor. The last Mughal emperor died in exile in 1862 at the age of 87.

After the disaster of 1857, the Company's rule in India was seen as highly inadequate, and corruption rose in its ranks. In truth, since the 1700s, the East India Company served the British government in ruling India as a non-official part of the British Empire. With the victory over the Indian rebels, the British politicians quit supporting the Company's rule of India and convinced Queen Victoria to take the title of "Empress of India." Through the Company, the British government inserted itself into the governance of India, and the abolishment of the East India Company was expected.

British Parliament passed the Government of India Act on August 2nd, 1858. The act formally dissolved the Company, and all its functions were transferred to the British Crown. A few months later, Queen Victoria proclaimed that all the people of India would be treated as subjects of the British Crown. The British government kept the bureaucracy of the East India Company, but it made a major shift when it came to the treatment of the Indian people. The new administration started a reform of the Indian government in which they tried to integrate the natives of higher castes and ex-rulers of the annexed kingdoms into the government itself. They also stopped all endeavors of Westernizing India, which meant the Christianization of the continent ended. A decree of religious tolerance was passed, and the Indians were allowed to step into the military service once more.

The British Raj was a construct that had the purpose, at least in part, to preserve the traditions and social hierarchy in India. The Crown often used this as an excuse for its rule over India. An investigation was conducted that concluded that the Company's efforts to introduce the free market to the conservative Indian society sabotaged the peasants, who were left at the mercy of merchants and local rulers.

Also, the Company failed to communicate with the local rulers and the common people. According to the British government, this was the main reason why the rebellions had happened in the first place. To serve as intermediaries between the British rule and the people, a new middle class of Indians was created. They were to be educated in new Indian universities and have guaranteed positions within the newly reorganized Indian government.

Although the East India Company was no more, the impact it had not just on the Indian subcontinent but also on the whole British Empire cannot be denied. The revenues the Company brought to the Crown allowed the expansion of British influence throughout the whole world, and the consequences of the Company's rule over India were both positive and negative. Their poor treatment of the natives led to the revolts that inspired India's fight for independence, but the Company did make it possible for Britain to become the leader of the Industrial Revolution, which, in turn, brought prestige and authority to the Crown.

Although the British often observed Indian culture as uncivilized and savage, many individuals of British descent fought to preserve it and keep it alive among the people who were ruled by a foreign power. For example, the first governor-general of India, Warren Hastings, learned the Pakistani and Urdu languages. He collected ancient Sanskrit manuscripts to preserve them, and he even hired locals to translate these manuscripts in English so he could make them available to the English-speaking world.

Chapter 3 – The Crown's Rule of India

The British Crown ruled the Indian subcontinent from 1858 after the East India Company was dissolved until 1947 when India gained its independence. The rule of Britain over India is better known as the British Raj. In both Sanskrit and Hindustani, "raj" means government or rule. Even though Queen Victoria proclaimed herself the empress of India in 1876, the British rule of the subcontinent was never officially named the Indian Empire.

It is important to make a difference between what we call India today and British India. The British Raj oversaw present-day India, Pakistan, and Bangladesh. Some places that are now under Indian control used to be the colonies of other European countries, like Goa, which was under Portuguese rule, and Pondicherry, which belonged to France. As Britain won and lost wars, other territories were included or excluded from the British Raj, such as Burma, British Somaliland, and Singapore.

The Crown rule of India was divided based on the type of territory. There were two types, British India and the princely states. British India was under direct British rule, while the princely states were ruled by the native rulers who were under British suzerainty. There were over 175 princely states, while British India was divided into provinces. The biggest difference between the provinces and the princely states was in their courts of law. While British India relied on laws that came from the British Parliament and the legislative power of the governor of India, some states were labeled as princely states, and they were still ruled by Indian royalty. The rulers of these vassal states had varying degrees of freedom, depending on their size and importance. Whatever aspects of the government they administered independently, communication and defense were always under British control.

Queen Victoria often used her title of the empress of India in her speeches and propaganda material, and she even started two orders of knighthood that were special to India: the senior "Most Exalted Order of the Star of India" in 1861 and the junior "Most Eminent Order of the Indian Empire" in 1878. The senior order stopped new appointments in 1947. The last member of the order, the maharaja of Alwar, died in 2009, and the order became inoperative. The junior order ceased to exist with the death of the maharaja of Dhrangadhra.

The Government

When the Indian Rebellion of 1857 was over, and after the Company was dismantled, the British Crown issued the Government of India Act. This led to a series of changes in how the subcontinent was governed from that point onward.

In London, a government department known as the India Office was opened in 1858. It was an executive branch of Britain's government, alongside the Foreign Office, the Colonial Office, the Home Office, and the War Office. The secretary of India had the assistance of the Council of India, whose members were chosen based on the years they had served in India. No person was allowed to join the council unless he spent at least ten years in India serving the Crown's interests. The civil servants who were employed in the India Office were organized into departments, a system taken directly from the administration of the East India Company. All the executive functions of the Company were now transferred to the secretary of India. He was in charge of superintendence, direction, and control of the provincial administrations in South Asia. However, the decisions made by the secretary were executed by the provincial viceroys and governors whose cabinets were in India. The British government maintained a tight grasp on the government of India; however, after the First World War, that grasp relaxed, allowing the local government to execute its own authority.

The India Office did not govern only the British Raj. In fact, under its control were all the British territories in Asia, Africa, and the Middle East. At different periods, it would also take control of the governing separate political entities of Bengal, Afghanistan, Zanzibar, Malaya, China, Japan, and others. It also regulated the interests of Indian migrants to the West Indies, Africa, and Fiji. In reality, the India Office continued to be what the East India Company once was. However, instead of sharing its profits made in the East Indies with the Crown, it was completely subjected to the Crown.

The secretary of India was a minister of the British Cabinet and the political head directly responsible for the governance of the British Raj. As the members of the East India Company already had the necessary experience in governing India, it was only natural to install them as the clerks who would serve the new office. Lord Edward Henry Stanley, who was the head of the board of the Company, took charge of the India Office. However, this branch was divided into two departments in 1937. One was tasked with governing the British Raj, and the other oversaw Aden (in today's Yemen) and Burma, though Lord Stanley maintained authority over both departments. In total, 27 individuals served as the secretary of India between 1858 and 1947, the year when India gained independence and the India Office was abolished. The next year, Burma followed the footsteps of the Indians and fought for its independence, making its office in London obsolete.

The Company had a governor-general office in Calcutta, and when the British Raj took over the rule, this position remained. However, the governor-general was now responsible to the secretary of India and, through him, to the British Parliament. This system of double government, one in London and one in Calcutta, had already existed under the rule of the East India Company, which had its Board of Control instead of the India Office. However, the upcoming years, which were the years of post-revolt reconstruction, brought changes to the Indian government. Before this, the governor-general had to consult the advisory council. Viceroy Lord Canning instead proposed that each member of the council should only deal with the tasks assigned to him. The collective decision-making route the Company had taken in the past was time-consuming and ineffective. The creation of separate departments for each of the counselors resulted in faster solutions to the pressing matters of the state. All the routine tasks of the government could be solved by the council members, but only the important issues needed the approval of the governor-general. However, the Executive Council still had the right to collectively decide what to do if the governor-general was absent. This innovation in the governance of India was decreed in 1861 in the Indian Councils Act.

The Executive Council could be expanded with the addition of a Legislative Council if the government of India needed to enact new laws. An additional twelve members would be added, and they would only be appointed for two years. Six of the new members were always chosen among the British officials, and they were the ones who had the right to vote when passing a new law. The other six were of Indian descent, and they only served as advisors. However, all the laws that the Legislative Council wanted to pass needed final approval by the secretary of India in London.

Even though the six members who were of Indian origin were added as a way to integrate the locals into the government of India, they were always chosen from a small pool of high-caste loyalists, and they were far from being the representatives of the will of the people. However, the true intention behind employing Indian representatives in the government was to change public opinion. These men were supposed to help appease the critiques of the government, both in Indian and British press, as their articles directly influenced public opinion.

In 1937, the Council of India was abolished and replaced with a similar council in London. This council had between eight and twelve members, and their task was to advise the secretary of India directly. All the members had to have served previously in India for at least ten years, and they had to have quit their offices in India no more than two years prior. The governor-general had the task of representing the Crown's interests in dealing with the princely states. However, in 1937, this task required a new department, and a new representative of the Crown was named. The Executive Council in India also had to be expanded to fourteen members by the time of the Second World War, with several new offices being founded.

The Indian Legislature consisted of an upper house and a lower house that represented the state council and the legislative assembly, respectively. The head of the upper house was the governor-general and the viceroy, while the assembly of the upper house was led by a president who would be elected for that position. The Council of State had 58 members in total, while the Legislative Assembly had 141 members. The president of the Legislative Assembly was appointed by the viceroy. This bicameral legislature had the power to make laws for everyone who resided in British India, no matter if they were of Indian or British descent. Also, the laws applied to the subjects of the British Raj who lived in other British colonies or the motherland.

With the Government of India Act of 1936, the new provinces of Sid and Orissa were created. A year later, the British Raj was divided into seventeen administrative territories, three of which were the Presidencies of Madras, Bombay, and Bengal. The other fourteen were known as the United Provinces, and they included the other provinces, including Punjab, Bihar, the Central Provinces and Berar, Orissa, Sind, and Delhi. All Presidencies and provinces were headed by a governor, and they all had their own legislatures. Each governor was a representative of the Crown and was assisted by ministers who were also the members of the provincial legislatures. All the actions of the provincial legislature had to be approved by the governor. The basic administrative units of the provinces were known as districts, and they were headed by a district magistrate. By 1947, the British Raj consisted of 230 districts in total.

Changes brought by the British Raj

Education

One of the most important changes the British Raj brought to India was in education. Thomas Macaulay, a member of the Council of India, spent four years reforming the education of the subcontinent based on the English model. He was the advocate of the Whig approach to historiography, which regarded the past as the progression toward liberty. He brought the ideas of the European Renaissance to India, such as the Scientific Revolution and the Enlightenment. Macaulay was dismissive toward the existing Indian culture, as he saw it as being inferior when compared to Western culture. In his view, the Indians were a stagnant nation that had fallen significantly behind the European scientific and philosophical ideas. He called his efforts at the reform of education the "civilizing mission." Some scholars today criticize Macaulay's "mission" as an excuse for the British rule to commit acts of racism since the government believed that Indians were not able to make any progress on their own and that they had to be ruled with an iron fist. However, other scholars think that the British truly believed that it was their moral obligation to bring enlightenment to India.

The East India Company opened universities in Calcutta, Bombay, and Madras just before the Rebellion of 1857. However, it wasn't the Company who opened the first education center in India. In 1542,

Saint Paul's College in Goa was opened by the European Jesuits, who also brought a printing press to the college so books could be spread easier throughout the subcontinent. The debate of the preferred language in which the classes of the new universities would be taught existed from the very beginning. The Orientalists thought that schools should teach in Indian languages, and they suggested either classical Sanskrit or Persian, which was the language of the Mughal courts. On the other side were the Anglicists, who wanted to introduce the English language in all schools in India, as modern India had nothing to teach their people.

The policy of introducing the English language in the education systems of the British colonies was enacted, and it is known as Macaulayism, named after its most prominent advocate. But this system only served the purpose of creating another layer in Indian society by introducing the class of anglicized Indians, who were nothing more than cultural intermediaries between the British and the Indians. The nationalist movement of India even blames Thomas Macaulay today for all the ills that came with colonization and for the creation of a new class that resents its heritage, and they strongly believe that it was the British people's way of imposing neocolonialism on India. Even today, the English language is used in Indian schools.

By 1911, the British government opened nearly 200 higher education facilities throughout India. They enrolled 36,000 pupils each year, of which 90 percent were men. After finishing university, the Indians were employed either in administrative services or as lawyers. This resulted in India having a well-educated professional state bureaucracy. However, the top civil service appointments were always reserved for the British who attended either Oxford or Cambridge. In 1939, the number of education facilities doubled, and the enrollment numbers jumped to 145,000 pupils per year. The Indian universities followed the curriculum set by Oxford and Cambridge, which meant they prioritized English literature and European history over India's.

Even though the British Raj opened many schools across India, literacy grew very slowly. At first, the British Raj only allowed higher education to Indians of high castes. Also, all education centers were concentrated in the bigger cities, with the countryside overlooked. In fact, before the 19th century, villages had their own educational institutions that taught their children useful skills, including reading and writing. However, the Company destroyed this system with its land control policies, and the village structure collapsed. India experienced an increase in literacy only after achieving independence in 1947. In modern times, especially in the period between 1991 and 2001, literacy in the subcontinent skyrocketed.

Agriculture and Industry

Some critics of the British rule of India would argue that the Crown was just an extension of the East India Company and that everything the British did in the territory of the continent was for their own gain. Even if this was true, it brought profits to India, as its GDP (gross domestic product) was raised to 57 percent, which was much better than the 27 percent achieved by the Company. However, the Indian population continuously grew, and the economic growth was not enough to boost the industry on its own, meaning some investments had to be made. To produce more, Indian agriculture had to be bolstered with a network of irrigation systems, the transportation of goods had to be improved, and Indian industries had to grow.

When it comes to agriculture, the British insisted on planting goods for export instead of food. Many fields were converted from food production to jute (a kind of fiber like hemp), cotton, sugarcane, coffee, tea, and opium. This conversion of food-growing fields into the production of raw materials, together with the Indian subcontinent's unpredictable climate, resulted in great famines. However, these exportable goods had the biggest impact on the growth of the national GDP. The demand for Indian raw materials was great, not just for the export industry but also for the domestic industry. India still had no competition in the textile industry since it produced the highest quality materials, which were always in high demand. Soon, the British realized they would have to expand the agricultural territories. But to turn territory into a fertile field, they needed to invest in irrigation systems.

By 1940, the British Raj had built many canals and irrigation systems in Uttar Pradesh, Bihar, Punjab, and Orissa. Many of these canals already existed due to the investments of the Mughal Empire, but they were badly maintained and needed modernization. The British extended the Ganges Canal, and it irrigated the territory of more than 350 miles. In Assam, the British cleared a jungle that occupied the territory of 1.62 hectares (4 acres), and it was converted into plantations, mainly for the production of tea.

Many of the irrigation systems that the British set into place served the purpose of watering the poppy plantations needed for the production of opium, which was mostly sold in China. The eastern and northern regions of India, namely the provinces of Behar, Rewa, and Awadh, were turned into poppy plantations. In 1850, the East India Company had poppy farms that occupied around 1,000 square kilometers (around 386 square miles). By 1900, the British Raj had doubled that number.

Besides canals and irrigation systems, the British Raj invested heavily in railways. The late 19th century saw the construction of a modern railway system that was renowned for its quality. It was also the fourth largest railway system in the world. The value of the railways lay in agriculture, military, and industry. The elaborate railway system ensured the safe and quick passage of raw materials to factories or ports, where the goods were shipped. The military used the railway for the quick transportation of troops and the movement of siege engines, weapons, and construction material needed for organized garrisons.

The funding for the railway system of India came from private British companies, and so, at first, private ownership of the railway was ensured. The Company first built the railway in 1832, and it was known as the Red Hill Railway. The British Raj expanded this network from an initial 32 kilometers (almost 20 miles) to 1,349 kilometers (a little over 838 miles) in 1860. By 1900, the railway network had grown to occupy a massive territory. During the British Raj, most of the construction of the railway was done by Indian companies, but the work was supervised by British engineers.

Both the First and Second World Wars crippled the Indian railway companies, as their production lines were converted into ammunition factories. A great number of trains were shipped to other colonies, depending on their needs. Without enough workers and facilities to produce both ammunition and railways, the tracks in some parts of India were stripped and shipped to the Middle East. The maintenance of the railroads was halted, and they quickly deteriorated.

Chapter 4 – The Famines of India

Victims of the famine of 1876–1878

https://en.wikipedia.org/wiki/File:India-famine-family-crop-420.jpg

Famines in India are a recurring thing, and they ravaged the subcontinent long before the British came. However, some of the most notorious famines happened during British rule, under both the East India Company and the British Raj. In the period between the 18th and early 20th centuries, around sixty million people died from starvation. It is believed that famines had such an impact on the population of India that they directly caused the long-term population growth in the subcontinent.

In India, to have a successful harvest, people had to rely on the summer monsoons, as they were responsible for filling the canals for irrigation with much-needed water. But droughts were not the only factor when it came to the great famines of India. The policies of the British Raj contributed to the worst famines that the Indian subcontinent ever saw. Many contemporary and modern critics blame the inactivity of the British government for the deaths of millions of people during the several famines that occurred between 1770 and 1943.

The British Raj adopted some of the policies developed by the East India Company, but many more were introduced under the Crown's rule of India. New war levies, rent taxes, a focus on exporting agricultural goods at the expense of food production, and the overall neglect of agricultural investments are some of the factors that directly influenced the severity of the famines in India. As stated above, the British economy relied on Indian goods, such as rice, indigo, cotton, jute, and opium. To increase the production of exported goods, millions of acres of land that had been used to bring domestic subsistence were displaced, leaving the Indians vulnerable to food shortages.

In 1866, a famine occurred in Odisha, and from there, it spread to Madras, Hyderabad, and Mysore, killing over a third of the population. Around 1,500 children were left orphaned, and the British offered three rupees per month to people who would take them in. The very next year, a famine in Rajasthan occurred, followed by Bengal (1873-1874), Deccan (1876-1878), and again in Madras, Hyderabad, Mysore, and Bombay (1876-1878). The famine forced people from these affected areas to migrate to those that had not been impacted yet. However, the bolstered number of people would cause another famine to break out, as there was simply not enough food to sustain them all.

The famines were followed by political controversy and discussions, which led to the foundation of the Indian Famine Commission that would later issue the Indian Famine Code. The code was developed in the 1880s after an extensive investigation was done after the Great Famine of 1876-78. The code was a famine scale, with three defined levels of food insecurity: near-scarcity, scarcity, and famine. If the crops failed for more than three years in a row, a scarcity level of food insecurity was proclaimed. Famine was defined both by crop failures and the increase of food prices to 140 percent above average. The famine level also included the migration of people due to a lack of food and heightened death tolls. The Indian Famine Codes were set to predict upcoming famines and therefore prevent them. Some of the policies of the Famine Codes included the rationing of food and the control of the food market during a possible outbreak.

In 1880, the Famine Commission concluded that each province of the British Raj had a surplus of food grains. The annual surplus, when added together, was 5.16 million metric tons. Bearing that in mind, the Commission came up with a series of policies that would regulate the response of the government to future famines. However, the governing viceroy of British Raj, Lord Robert Bulwer-Lytton, opposed any efforts to relieve the famine in India, as he believed the Indian workers would stop performing their duties, which would, in the end, result in the bankruptcy of India. He was strictly against government meddling in the reduction of food prices, and he even ordered district offices to discourage and disrupt any relief works that might happen. He referred to the Indian famines dismissively, saying, "Mere distress is not a sufficient reason for opening a relief work."

Previously, in 1874, famine had broken out in Bengal, and Sir Richard Temple, the lieutenant-governor of the region, successfully intervened. The mortality rate of this famine was very low, but Sir

Temple was criticized extensively by other British officials for spending too much money on famine relief. When Madras started being affected by a new famine only two years later, Lord Lytton did nothing to help ease the situation. This resulted in around five and a half million deaths, and Lytton was finally convinced to introduce a policy in which the financial surplus would be spent on relief efforts. Even though the measure was fairly lax, the British officials were satisfied, and they all complied with it. As one might be able to predict, another famine broke out, this time in 1896, and the measures were not enough to help the suffering people, as around 4.5 million people died of starvation. Unfortunately, it was as if the British rulers learned nothing. George Curzon, the viceroy of India between 1899 and 1905, continued to criticize any relief plans, and he considered the rations to be too high. His actions directly led to the deaths of millions of people, with some estimates as high as ten million.

The threat of famine was constant in India until 1902. There were no major famine outbreaks in India until 1943, which was when one of the most devastating famines in Bengal occurred. It took between 2.5 and 3 million lives. The Famine Commission identified that the cause of the famine was the lack of employment for agricultural workers. Therefore, a strategy was created to find work for these people. The Indian Famine Codes were used even after the independence of the Indians, and even more lessons were learned during the famine in 1966-67. The Indian government updated the codes and renamed them the Scarcity Manuals, which are still used today.

One of the criticisms of the government's handling of the famines in India came from a famous British nurse, Florence Nightingale, who pointed out that it wasn't the lack of food in a particular geographic area that caused the famine but rather the lack of transportation. She blamed the inadequate transportation of food on the complete absence of a political and social structure in India. She went further by identifying two types of famine: a grain famine and a money famine. The first one was caused by crop failures, but the other one was caused by the decisions the British government made while ruling India.

After all, the British had destroyed the structure of a traditional village in India. All land was now owned by the magnates, and the peasants had to rent the land they worked. This drained the money from the peasants to fill the pockets of the landowners, and it made it impossible for the peasants to afford food. Also, the money that should have been used to produce food was used for other purposes. Nightingale pointed out that the British Raj spent too much money on the military, and that same money should be put toward food production.

The same opinion was later voiced by Amartya Sen, the Nobel Prize winner of Economic Sciences in 1998. He, too, criticized the British government of India, blaming them for the inadequate transportation of food from unaffected areas to the areas undergoing famine. But it wasn't only the distribution of food that failed during the famines of the 1870s. The incorporation of grain into the grain market through the use of railways and telegraphs was almost nonexistent. The rails were already in place and managed well, but instead of the government using them to distribute the food to the affected areas, they were used by merchants, who transported their grain to facilities, allowing them to hoard the shipments. Telegraph lines were not used to communicate the reduction of the prices of grain on the market. Instead, they were used to coordinate the price increase, thus making the food unavailable to low-caste workers.

It was only after the Indian Famine Codes of 1880 that the railway started being used to transport the food surplus from an unaffected area to one that was experiencing famine. The Famine Commission also urged the government to expand the railway system inland. Up until that point, the main railway system was concentrated around important port cities that were used for exporting goods. The new lines were constructed, and they served the purpose of allowing food to flow to all regions that were affected by famine. However, even though the railroads ensured that food reached famine-affected areas, they could not ensure that hungry people would be able to actually buy the food. The Famine Commission relied on famine relief efforts provided by the government and did little to ensure the accessible prices of food on the market.

The railway system of India also served the purpose of transporting people from affected areas, sometimes even transporting them outside of India. The migrations, together with the famine relief efforts, was just enough to soften the blow of a mid-scale shortage of food. However, the migration brought new problems. Famine weakens a person's immune response, and many diseases, such as cholera, malaria, dysentery, and smallpox, took more lives than hunger itself. By migrating in search of food, people would bring these diseases to other areas, causing an epidemic. It was only after gaining its independence that India included the fight against infectious diseases in the Scarcity Manuals.

The Great Famine of 1876–78

The Madras Famine in 1877

https://en.wikipedia.org/wiki/Famine_in_India#/media/
File:Madras_famine_1877.jpg

In 1876, a great famine occurred when the crops failed in the Deccan Plateau. The cause of this famine can be found in the particularly long drought that happened due to the interaction between El Niño and the Indian Ocean Dipole, which is when the western part of the Indian Ocean has higher surface temperatures than its eastern part. The result of this weather phenomenon was a widespread drought, not just in India but also in certain areas of China, South America, and Africa. As a consequence of the drought, a famine occurred, in which between nineteen and fifty million people died.

In India, the famine was severe mainly because the British Raj decided to continue with the export of grain as if nothing was happening. It is recorded that during the two years of the Great Famine, 320,000 tons of wheat were exported just to England alone. The viceroy who decided to continue with the export was, as one might suspect, Lord Robert Bulwer-Lytton. His tenure as a viceroy was largely seen as very productive, and so, the public often turned a blind eye to his ruthlessness in dealing with the Great Famine, as well as the Second Anglo-Afghan War (1878–1880).

During the famine of Bihar (1873–1874), a high death toll was avoided due to the imported rice from Burma. However, the government wasn't satisfied with the high expenses of the famine relief, and it was decided that the British Raj should lower its spending on welfare. The lieutenant-governor of Bengal, Sir Richard Temple, was the man responsible for the decision of importing rice, and during the Great Famine, he occupied the position of famine commissioner for the government of India. But because Temple had previously received strong criticism for his spending on famine relief, he was reluctant to do anything about the famine in 1876. During the Great Famine, Temple insisted that the government should not meddle in transactions done by private parties, and he also implemented strict standards for the eligibility to receive help during the famine. By his standards, only very small children, the extremely poor, and the elderly were eligible for charity during the famine, while everyone else was to be provided with "relief work." The work for able-bodied men, women, and children often meant relocation to the areas where labor workers were needed the most.

The measures that the British government undertook to relieve India of the Great Famine were not enough. In fact, they were so strict and inadequate that they inspired protests in Bombay. Those who were given "relief work" were paid less, and they were stationed in the relief camps near Madras and Bombay, living in very poor conditions. The payment of the relief workers usually came in the form of food, which would have been appreciated during the famine if it didn't consist of only one pound of grain and nothing else. Women and children received even less. If there was money involved for payments during the famine, men would earn one-sixteenth of a rupee, with women and children earning less.

Some people in the British government of India opposed these low wages for "relief work," and they demanded that the rations be increased and that some form of protein and vitamins be included in the meal, be it meat or vegetables. However, the reasoning behind the low wages was the belief that any excessive charity would lead to the Indian people becoming too dependent on government help and that the productivity of the workers would fall.

The pressure of the opposition did lead to an increase of relief, though, and protein was also added to the rations. But these new measures were implemented only in March 1877, which came too late for the many people who had already died of hunger. The fact that this government help came too late is also supported by statistics, which testify that, during the second year of the Great Famine, more people died of the malaria pandemic than from hunger itself. Even though a year earlier the famine commissioner had proclaimed that the famine was under control, the people continued to suffer and die throughout 1878, either directly from hunger or from the consequences of malnutrition.

The Bengal Famine of 1943

The Bengal province is mainly agricultural, with rice being the most important crop. In fact, the land of the Bengal province is covered with fields that produce a third of the rice that comes from India. Eighty percent of the arable land is covered in rice fields, which is also the main food for this region, next to fish. However, rice-rich Bengal continuously stagnated in food production while its population was growing. Soon enough, there was not enough food for both exportation and the locals. On top of that, the crops failed in 1942 during the peak of the Second World War.

According to the census from 1941, Bengal had approximately sixty million people living there. The growth in population is largely due to improved living standards and healthcare, which lowered the mortality rate. And even though the people of Bengal were mostly farmers, they produced the lowest amount of food in the world. This is due to the government's low investment in the area; thus, the Bengali people were forced to use underdeveloped agricultural equipment and the old methods of working the land. Of course, the government offered various types of credit to the people who owned the land or who were renting it; however, no peasant was able to afford a state loan that would help him develop his production.

With the rise of the population in Bengal, a need for more arable land arose. To acquire new land for food production, large forests had to be cut down. This caused the drainage of the soil, as the natural channels that supplied it with water were disrupted. New canals had to be constructed to replace the natural ones, and entire river flows had to be moved. But the government wasn't as interested in investing in the region as much as in exploiting it. Some deforestation projects ended up abandoned, and the demand for food could not be met.

By 1930, the Bengali region had transformed from one of the biggest exporters of rice to a region that needed to import food to sustain its population. On top of the shortage of food, there's some evidence that Bengalis ate the least nutritious food in India. The population mostly ate rice, which in those times wasn't enriched with macronutrients as it is today. The result was a malnourished populace who often suffered various infectious diseases due to the weak immune response of their bodies.

There is one more factor that influenced not only the start of the Bengal famine but also the efforts of its relief. The Bengal region saw railway construction during 1890, but that same construction led to changed river flows. In the 1940s, the areas that should have been naturally flooded were dry, and the fields that should have been dry experienced too much water. The changed river flows and the disruption of the irrigation systems due to the railway construction resulted in crop failures. However, the new railroad was mainly used for military purposes and not so much for food transport. The Bengali roads were in bad condition, as they were poorly maintained, and the British Raj mainly relied on river transportation to supply Bengal with much-needed food. However, the rivers were disrupted too much, and the food couldn't reach all the areas affected by the food shortage. The newly flooded areas were also particularly fertile grounds for waterborne infectious diseases like cholera and malaria, which additionally weakened the people of Bengal.

The already swollen population of Bengal was on the brink of economic disaster when the Japanese invaded Burma in 1942. Many people fleeing the war came to Bengal as refugees, placing additional stress on the region's agriculture and economy. Unfortunately, the Burmese refugees brought diseases such as smallpox and dysentery with them, resulting in thousands of deaths. Now, the already hungry population was facing a shortage of medicine as well.

Once Japan invaded Burma, the Bengal province became the first line of defense. The territory became flooded with military convoys, and the unskilled labor of the Bengalis was often used to build airports for the Allied forces that fought in the Second World War. The military needs strained the economy of the province even more, not just because of the great number of soldiers who came and needed to be fed but also because the locals were often displaced from their lands to work at military construction sites. Their land was often purchased for small amounts of money so it could be used for military camps, bases, and airports. This meant that a province that barely had enough food to sustain itself now lost the land that produced the food. The need for imports was growing, but there was no money to buy imported food, and there was also no means of fast and safe transportation for that food.

The province of Bengal was already facing famine when, in 1942, the government made a series of decisions that would directly lead to millions of deaths. The so-called "denial policy" was instated to deny the surplus of crops in certain provinces so the Japanese couldn't take it. Instead of distributing the surplus crops to the regions that faced famines, they were ordered to be destroyed. Later investigations showed that this policy increased corruption. The amount of food that was confiscated as surplus was far greater than it should have been, and instead of being destroyed as ordered, it was exported and sold for a much higher price. Another "denial policy" restricted the size of boats that were allowed to sail on the Bengali rivers. Any boat that could potentially carry more than ten individuals was destroyed. This meant that boats that would have been able to transport food were denied access to the Bengali rivers or were simply destroyed in fear of the invading Japanese.

However, on the local level, the provincial government started opening the gruel kitchens. At first, they didn't know how to react, and they delayed offering any relief to their famine-stricken citizens. In August 1943, the distribution of gruel started, but it didn't have enough nutritional value for survival. The grains served as food were often too old, moldy, and contaminated with pathogens that only caused new diseases to rise. Nevertheless, these gruel kitchens offered some hope and bought time for the government to react. Various national and international groups, such as communists, women's groups, merchant's guilds, and groups of citizens, sent donations of food, money, and clothes. However, they were simply not enough. Finally, in October of 1943, the new viceroy of Bengal, Archibald Wavell, brought military envoys that worked tirelessly on repairing the railroads and distributing the food to all parts of Bengal, no matter how remote they were. The food was brought from Punjab, which also sent medical relief teams. Thus, the healing of Bengal started. The very next season, Bengal had the largest rice yield ever harvested. But there were not enough survivors to collect the harvest, and the soldiers had to offer their help once more. But the work was far from over. Viceroy Wavell had much to do to protect the citizens of Bengal from going through the same suffering in the future. He made several political decisions that put pressure on Britain to increase the import of food to India. By January 1944, the famine in Bengal was officially over.

Chapter 5 – Nationalism in India

The Indian National Congress

In order to justify its government of India, Britain created a new middle class of well-educated Indians, whose employment in the government secured pro-Western and pro-British views of the local Indian population. They attended schools opened by the British government, and they were eager to get involved in politics with the goal of modernizing Indian legislation, economy, and society. After the Indian Rebellion of 1857, and throughout the 1860s and 1870s, the national awareness of the educated Indian middle class grew. It finally culminated in 1885 with the foundation of the Indian National Congress.

However, the educated Indians were well aware that they were under foreign rule and that they needed the help of British officials to be heard. Luckily, they had a retired British official named Allan Octavian Hume on their side. Together, they created an Indian National Union, which would work jointly with the British government. The Union had the task of being a mediator between the British government and the Indian people. They were the ones who made sure that the government heard the people's opinion. With the British general elections coming up in 1885, the Indian National Union called upon the British people to give their votes to the candidates who best voiced their concerns about the social and political position of the Indians. They encouraged the people to vote against the taxation of Indians to finance British wars, and they gave their open support to the legislative reforms in India. However, the movement of the Indian National Union was a complete failure. The new Indian middle class finally realized that they could not expect the help of the British officials and that they had to fight their political battles alone.

So, on December 28th, 1885, the Indian National Congress was formed. Hume remained a supporter of the movement, which had now grown into a political party, and he assumed the position of general secretary. The first president of the party was Womesh Chunder Bonnerjee, an attorney from Calcutta. The first session of the new political party had 72 delegates in attendance, among them only two British members with the rest being Indians.

The Indian National Congress wasn't the first nationalist effort of the Indian people to have a say in the politics of the British government. There were many movements that came before the establishment of the political party, but they all lacked recognition. These nationalist campaigns had been mostly active in the political scene of India since 1875. For instance, the Indians protested cotton imports, as they wanted the textile industry to remain completely within India. The years of 1877 and 1878 saw the demand of Indianization of government services, as well as the opposition to the British efforts in Afghanistan. Many Indian presses supported the nationalist movements. In 1883, the *Indian Mirror* of Calcutta started its continuous campaign of promoting the need for an all-Indian political entity in the government. This campaign lasted until 1885 when the Indian National Congress was founded.

Among the first difficulties the Indian National Congress faced was the fact that Indians didn't have the same kind of unity that was generally observed in other nations around the world. This is because India was never really a nation; it was a mere geographical term for the territories of the subcontinent. The Indians had to be united, and they had to be given a national identity. They were a nation-in-the-making, a congress of hundreds of different races, cultures, and castes. The end goal of the Indian National Congress was the modernization of the Indian society. However, modernization doesn't equal Westernization. Even though the new middle class of India was pro-Western and had a British mindset, they were well aware that India was not a part of the Western world.

However, this attitude of the Indian National Congress instigated negative critique by some of the major religious groups of India. Muslims, traditional Hindus, and some religions practiced by the minority regarded the modernization of India as a breakaway from tradition and the "good old days." The past was often considered to be the golden age of the Indian subcontinent, and any attempt of modernization was regarded as Westernization and the promotion of the British culture.

Because India wasn't (and still isn't) a homogenous country, the political structure of the government and the methods used to get there had to be different. The Indian National Congress made a rule in the session of 1888 to not pass a resolution that was opposed by an overwhelming majority of Hindu or Muslim delegates. This rule was an attempt to reach out to the cultural and religious minorities in India. In 1889, the Indian National Congress added a minority clause to the resolution in which they demanded legislative reform. The clause stated that the percentage of Parsis, Christians, Muslims, or Hindus elected to the legislative council was not to be less than their proportion in the population.

The Indian National Congress created a common political program for all Indians. This meant that they would fight only for the rights and issues that were common to the native Indian population. The leaders of the political party understood that India was a multicultural subcontinent and that it would be an impossible battle if they were to fight for social reforms that would please every cultural group and sub-group that existed in India. This is why the Indian National Congress focused its political agenda on civil rights, administration, and the economy of India and its influence on the indigenous people of the subcontinent.

The Indian National Congress was made up of the educated middle class of India and had an elitist attitude. The leaders and members of the political party were often too concerned with how they would be accepted in the British government that they never really bothered to make their existence known to the common people of India. The political agenda of the party was also too concerned with more mundane political issues, such as the number of Indian representatives in the British Parliament and the freedom of speech for Indian politicians. While these issues were definitely important, other more pressing issues should have been addressed first, issues that affected everyone in India, such as the healthcare system, poverty, and the social oppression that the Indians suffered under the British Raj.

The Swadeshi Movement

In 1905, the British government decided to divide Bengal to raise the efficiency of its administration. Bengal was the largest province of India, and at that point, it had over 78 million people. The division separated the eastern and western parts of Bengal, but it wasn't just a territorial division. The Muslims in the east were now separated from their Hindu countrymen in the west. With the nationalist movement of India on the rise, the division was largely seen as an attempt of the British government to divide the singular country to rule it more effortlessly. They were afraid that the British rulers sought to turn the nations of India against each other.

The British government of India only wanted to achieve administrative efficiency with this division, but in turn, they created two separate nationalist movements in India that would continue to fight foreign rule throughout the decades to come. One was the Swadeshi movement of the Hindus, and the other one was the All-

India Muslim League. However, even modern historians believe that the partition of Bengal had some political agenda behind it. Calcutta was the seat of the Indian National Congress, which had gained in popularity and presented a thorn to British politics in the subcontinent. In an attempt to displace the political party, the British government only managed to instigate nationalism in India, which would take the shape of terrorism, as the students opted for bombings and shootings to achieve their goals.

Before the partition of Bengal, the Indian National Congress started petitions against it but to no avail. A more aggressive approach was needed, and the Indian National Congress started calling all the people of India to boycott British products. The result of this call was unexpected, and the nationalist movement of India made a huge step forward by involving both rural and urban populations of Bengal into the state of politics. Suddenly, women and students started being politically active as well as the commoners. The nationalist movement of India grew from an elitist group to a popular crusade. The division of the nation managed what the Indian National Congress had been trying to achieve for decades, and the nation of India was finally united under a common goal, to oppose the foreign rule of Britain.

The Swadeshi movement took its name from Sanskrit, and it is nothing more than the conjugation of the words *Swa*, which means self or own, and *desh*, which means country. Therefore, Swadeshi means "one's own country." In the eyes of the members of the movement, Bengal was interpreted as the Goddess Kali, who had been abused by the British. In Hinduism, Kali is seen as the destroyer of evil, and as such, she was the patron goddess of many movements in India, whether they were religious, social, or political. Their rallying cry was "Vande Mataram," "Hail the mother(land)." The Swadeshi movement had the support of other regions of India, and protests supporting them were organized in Poona, Punjab, Bombay, Delhi, Kangra, Jammu, and Haridwar.

Officially, the Swadeshi movement was proclaimed on August 7th, 1905, in the meeting of the Indian National Congress in Calcutta. The movement gained political leadership and a more direct focus when the decision to boycott all British products was made. The leaders of the movement toured the country to spread the word of the boycott. In some places, they even gathered crowds of tens of thousands of people. As a result, Manchester cloth and Liverpool salt recorded a fall of sales by 5 to 15 percent in just the first year of the boycott.

In time, the Swadeshi movement would create a division inside the Indian National Congress, as part of the political party wanted to resort to more extreme measures, while the rest wanted to continue with their peaceful approach. In 1906, the Congress declared that their new goal was the self-government of India. In India, self-governance was known as Swaraj. The Indian National Congress was divided into Moderates, who were not ready for such a radical move as Swaraj, and the Extremists, who sought to speed up the process of creating an all-Indian government.

The boycott moved from refusing to buy, sell, and consume foreign products to an overall refusal of everything British, including schools, courts, titles, and government services. The goal was to make the administration of the Indian subcontinent impossible for the British government and to lessen the exploitation of the Indian territories, which only served to help British commerce. The British government saw the resignation of a large number of Indian officials, such as constables, deputies, clerks, and even sepoys. On the other hand, some of the members of the Swadeshi Movement opted for the use of violence to fight the British government. However, it was the boycott of the foreign goods that had the best results.

However, in 1908, the movement experienced a cooling phase. It ultimately failed, largely because it didn't manage to engage the Muslim population, especially in the countryside. The British government observed the Swadeshi movement as a threat, and it came down on it with a heavy hand. To demotivate the movement, the government banned all public gatherings, processions, and press. Students who participated in the movement rallies were expelled from colleges, and the government officials who supported the movement were removed from their offices. People were often beaten up by the police, and they faced fines that were impossible for commoners to pay.

Even though the Swadeshi movement declined, it did bring up ideas that would only serve to reinforce Indian nationalism. The movement left its trail in the culture of India through literature, song, and storytelling, and these continued to spread throughout the Indian subcontinent, even though the movement achieved little to nothing. The Swadeshi movement was only the beginning of the Indian struggle against British colonialism, though. The ideas behind it would continue to exist, and it would be newly awakened in the future through the efforts of Mahatma Gandhi.

The All-India Muslim League

Just as with Hindus, the British Raj failed to incorporate Muslims and their teachings into the new social structure of India. Even though the Muslim educational centers were open, they focused on the British curriculum and sciences. This created a response from Muslim scholars, who advocated for Islamic teachings and who opposed the notion that all citizens of India, both Muslim and Hindu, had to be Westernized. The national identity of Muslims was indeed present much earlier than that of Hindus; however, their preoccupation with the preservation of their culture and religion diverted them from fully entering the political scene.

All-India Muslim League conference

The efforts to preserve Muslim education, culture, and religion were impossible without certain special rights that needed to be obtained from the British government. The need for a separate political party was obvious, and some individuals among the Muslim scholars organized themselves into a political party known as the All-India Muslim League. The League was formed in Dhaka, Bangladesh, in December 1906. It was formed a year after the partition of Bengal occurred, as the event only sped up the creation of the League since it concentrated Muslims into the eastern territories of the province and elevated their sense of a separate nation.

The founder of the All-India Muslim League, Nawab Khwaja Salimullah, wasn't elected as its first president. The honor of that position belonged to another founder of the League, Sir Sultan Muhammad Shah (Aga Khan III). Both Salimullah and Muhammad Shah were patrons of Muslim education in India, and they both strongly believed that Muslims needed an educational capital before indulging in politics. They fought for the opening of a Muslim university in Dhaka, but it was not until 1911 that they would succeed. The annulment of the partition of Bengal by King George V was performed that year, and the All-Muslim League became even more concerned about the interests of Muslims in the area of education. It was only when they voiced their concerns after the reunification of Hindu and Muslim Bengal that they were granted permission to open a Muslim university in Dhaka.

One of the first things the All-India Muslim League demanded after its creation was separate representation in the British government, and their first victory toward this goal happened in 1908 when the House of Lords accepted their proposal. However, the League was unsatisfied with the number of seats that were to be reserved for Muslim representatives in Parliament. The very next year, Muslims protested the government's decision, and to make a compromise, more seats were given to Muslim representatives.

The Muslims and Hindus found a common language during World War I, as both groups had similar rights to fight for. There was even an attempt to form a Muslim-Hindu alliance; however, once the war ended, this alliance wouldn't live for long. The Muslims and Hindus grew apart, with each group turning back to their community. The Muslims were outraged that the Ottoman Empire had been placed under sanctions after World War I, and they organized riots across India that were meant to display their support to the Ottoman Empire. Many Muslim politicians even left their positions in the government. The All-India Muslim League recognized that the British "two-nations in one state" belief (that Muslims and Hindus could live together in one state) was impossible to maintain, and the League changed their agenda from advocating for Muslim rights within India to the creation of an all-Muslim state in the Indian subcontinent. The idea of Pakistan was born, but the British government strongly opposed it. For the British Raj, India had to be one political entity, not just because of the administration but also because of the economic gains. If Muslims had their own state, Britain would be forced to treat them as a separate economic entity as well.

During the 1940s, the All-India Muslim League grew, attracting over two million members. However, their political views became more and more influenced by religion. They could not see a reason to stay united with the Hindus, with whom they shared nothing in common. Their cultures, language, literature, and history were completely different, and as such, they believed that the two nations couldn't possibly live under the same government. The sentiment for separatism grew exponentially. However, not all Muslims felt this way. Some declared it would be best for all social groups to remain united under one state. When the All-India Muslim League passed the resolution to create a new state, they were opposed by other Muslim groups, such as the All India Azad Muslim Conference. The violent conflict was inevitable, and the leader of the Azad Muslim Conference, Allah Bakhsh Soomro, was murdered.

The new Muslim state of Pakistan would contain the provinces of Sindh, Punjab, Baluchistan, the Northwest Frontier Province, and Bengal. The declaration of the resolution of the All-India Muslim League led to even more violent conflicts, especially in the aforementioned provinces. Instead of suing for peace, the League financed their supporters, who rallied and protested, often creating unrest and committing violence against Hindus and Sikhs.

However, there was nothing the League could do to gain the support for Pakistan within the British government. Only after the British rule of India ended in 1947 could the new state be created. Even then, the League couldn't agree on the future of their new state, and it became divided into smaller political parties with different ideologies. Later, the All-India Muslim League would reunite, this time under a different name, the Pakistan Muslim League.

Chapter 6 – India during World War I

Indian bicycle troops at the Battle of the Somme

https://en.wikipedia.org/wiki/Indian_Army_during_World_War_I#/media/
File:Indian_bicycle_troops_Somme_1916_IWM_Q_3983.jpg

The Ghadar Movement

Since 1904, the West Coast of North America had been an attractive migration destination for many Indians, especially those from the Punjab area. The hunger, poverty, and lack of opportunities forced Indians to seek employment in other states, and while the British government was satisfied to let the Indians work on their plantations in Fiji and Burma, they were against migration to North America, where socialist ideas of freedom were on the rise. By 1908, the secretary of state of India even implemented restrictions on immigration to Canada because he was afraid that if Indians met the free Western world, the British government would lose the prestige by which they ruled India. The British Raj did not need to use force during their rule over this issue, as Indians believed they were a part of a greater empire.

Despite the restrictions, some Indians managed to emigrate to Canada and the western states of the United States. They were veteran soldiers of the British Indian Army, and since they had fought around the world, they already knew of the prosperity of the Western world. Even though these men and their families faced harsh racism and scrutiny in the West, they chose to stay, as the poverty and hunger back home was the only other option. Shunned away from the predominantly white communities of Canada and America, Indians organized themselves into tight-knit groups, where they allowed their nationalistic ideas to grow. However, instead of fighting for their rights in the lands where they found themselves, they focused their efforts on the situation back home in India. They felt that as long as they were not free in India, they could not expect other nations to treat them as equals.

Various Indian nationalistic movements started popping up in the West, and they even organized newspapers that promoted their separatist ideas, such as *Circular-e-Azadi* in San Francisco or *Free Hindustan* in Vancouver. Indian immigrants remembered the Swadeshi movement, and they pledged their support to it. Some political exiles from India found their new homes in Canada and the US, where they continued to promote their ideas of overthrowing British rule. The first to preach a violent revolution against the British was a Sikh priest named Bhagwan Singh, who came to the West in 1913, just before the start of the First World War.

Bhagwan Singh was banished from Canada, and he moved to the US, where the political teachings of Lala Har Dayal had already gathered Indian immigrants into one community. Har Dayal was a professor at Stanford University, but his efforts to help immigrant workers in the US led him to politics. After the attempted assassination of Lord Charles Hardinge, the viceroy of India, in 1912, Har Dayal realized that there was a possibility for a revolutionary overthrow of the British government, and he moved his focus from workers' syndicates for immigrants in the US to the preaching of an armed and violent uprising in India. He founded the Hindi Association in Portland and started preaching to the immigrant Indians to go back home and call their countrymen to take up arms against the British. The ideas of Har Dayal were quickly accepted by the immigrants, and a new publication, the *Hindustan Ghadar*, was issued weekly, calling for revolution. As one might surmise, the Ghadar movement got its name from this publication.

The onset of World War I didn't stop the plans of the Ghadar movement. In fact, they saw it as an opportunity to plant the seeds of revolution among the Indian soldiers, who would, in turn, fight against the British instead of beside them. They spread their propaganda not just among the immigrants in the US and Canada but also to the Indians working in the Malay States, Fiji, the Philippines, China, and Japan, calling them to go back home and instigate a revolution.

But the Ghadar movement didn't keep their revolution a secret, which was a grave mistake. Instead of silently organizing the revolt back home, their propaganda was very loud, and it circulated the world. Once the movement was ready to take action, the British government in India was ready for them. The first immigrants who returned to Indian soil were apprehended. Those who were recognized as being less dangerous were confined to their villages under strict orders not to leave them. The more dangerous immigrants, though, were arrested. However, many Ghadar members managed to arrive in India undetected, and they proceeded to Punjab, where they planned to start their revolution.

Unfortunately for them, the Punjab they hoped to return to was different from what they expected. Even though the Ghadar movement propaganda had reached them, the citizens were passive and simply had no interest in revolution. The leaders of the movement tried their best to spark nationalism in their fellow Indians but to no avail. Some of the Punjab citizens started reporting the Ghadar leaders, which led to their arrests. Aware that they were being received with scorn, the Ghadars tried to spread their influence through the ranks of the sepoys. Although they were successful at instigating small-scale mutinies among the soldiers, they lacked centralized leadership, which would allow them to focus their efforts more clearly.

The leaders of the Ghadar movement had also just returned from spending many years in Canada, the US, and even Germany, which made them unpopular among the locals. They quickly became aware that they needed someone familiar, someone who already proved his worth to the territory of India, if they were to inspire the citizens. The very next year, in 1915, Rash Behari Bose answered their call and accepted the leadership of the Ghadar movement. Bose was already very popular among the Indians who were against colonial rule, as he was the one who had attempted the assassination of Viceroy Lord Charles Hardinge in 1912.

With this new leadership, the Ghadar movement improved their communication and organization. Bose sent men to various military garrisons with the task of spreading the word of the upcoming mutiny and recruiting willing sepoys. On February 11th, 1915, the scouts returned, bearing optimistic reports, and the Ghadar movement set the date of the uprising for February 21ˢᵗ. However, an agent of the Criminal Investigation Department managed to infiltrate the movement, and he notified the government of Bose's plans. The Ghadar members sensed something was up, and they decided to speed up the mutiny and move it to February 19ᵗʰ. However, the undercover agent was not caught, and he brought the new details to the government, which was more than ready to take action against the movement.

Most of the Ghadar leaders were arrested, although Bose managed to escape, and the mutiny was crushed even before it had started. The government wanted to set an example to prevent any future organizations attempting similar efforts as the Ghadar movement. Punjab and Mandalay (Burma) saw an excessive number of conspiracy trials that sentenced 45 revolutionaries to death, with over 200 sentenced to prison. The government's retaliation left India without an entire generation of nationalist leaders in Punjab.

However, the failure of the Ghadar movement didn't discourage all revolutionaries. Some still operated, especially the Indian migrants in Berlin and the US under the leadership of Ram Chandra. With the help of the German government, which was eager to dispose of British supremacy, they continued to make attempts to instigate mutinies. They succeeded in inspiring violent opposition to British rule, but it only took place in a few locations, and there were not enough numbers to start a widespread Indian revolt. Even though the Ghadar movement failed to make a significant political change in India, what it did do was keep the spirit of nationalism alive and remind civilians of the Swadesh ideology and that self-governance of India could be attained if enough people united.

The Home Rule Movement

In 1909, Bal Gangadhar Tilak, an Indian nationalist and independence activist, was exiled from India and sentenced to spend the next six years in a prison in Mandalay, Burma. He was accused of organizing protests and holding speeches against the British government on three separate occasions, in 1897, 1902, and later in 1916. Tilak was a member of the Indian National Congress, and he had belonged to the Extremists when the Congress split into two in 1907. In 1915, he was back in India, and he wanted to rejoin the Congress and mend the split between the Extremists and Moderates. To do so, he made a public declaration, in which he made a comparison between the Irish Home Rule movement and the nationalist Indians. Tilak believed that Indians should seek to reform the administrative system and not overthrow the government, which had happened in Ireland. He also publicly condemned all the violent attacks on the British that had happened under the influence of the Ghadar movement. He offered his full support to the British Crown, and he urged all Indians to offer their help to the government in the wake of World War I.

The Indian National Congress proved to be very sympathetic toward Tilak, especially because they were pressured by another important political character that vigorously worked on the reformation of India, Mrs. Annie Besant. She joined the Congress in 1914 and was keen to wake up the dormant party and push it to national political activity.

At the time, Annie Besant was 66 years old, but her political career had started back in England during her youth. She became aware of the situation of the poor in England after her marriage when she was twenty. Soon, she learned about the English radicals and the Union of Farmers, who demanded better working conditions. Besant clashed with her husband, who had different political ideas than her, and the couple split after only six years of marriage. She then enrolled in the Birkbeck Literary and Scientific Institution, which was where she started her activism work in the area of religion and politics. She was the most active in areas such as women's rights, birth control, secularism, socialism, and worker's rights. Besant actually shared her ideas with Irish writer George Bernard Shaw, with whom she grew very close to and possibly started a relationship. However, divorces were unavailable to a woman of middle-class status in 19th-century England, and she remained the legal wife of her previous husband, who condemned her love affair with the Irish writer. Besant started to show interest in the occult and became a member of the Theosophical Society. This occult society sought to make a connection between various religions, and it found inspiration in Hindu, Buddhism, and Sufi teachings, as well as in Christianity. It was this society that brought Annie Besant to India in 1893, where she became interested in the social problems of castes and foreign rule.

Once she joined the Indian National Congress in 1914, her attention switched from social activism to building a home rule similar to the Irish Home Rule movement. To do this, she needed the support of both the Extremists and Moderates, and she worked hard with Tilak on mending the wounds caused by the party split. They were successful, and the Congress reunited both factions into one political party. However, their success was partial, as the Moderates of the Bengal wing of the Indian National Congress did not allow the Extremists to rejoin their midst.

During 1915, Annie Besant launched a campaign in which she called for public meetings and conferences to demand the self-government of India. Her actions, and those of Tilak, changed the minds of the leaders of the Bengal wing of the Indian National Congress, and finally, the party was made whole again. However, Besant had no luck in attracting the Congress and the Muslim League to her idea of setting up a home rule. Tilak was attracted to her idea, though, and he took the initiative and set up his own home rule league in Bombay. Since the Indian National Congress remained passive regarding self-government, in September 1916, Besant left them to set up her home rule league, and she gained many followers. The two separate home rule leagues existed at the same time as each other, but they avoided conflicts by setting up in the territories in which they would be active. Tilak's league worked in the areas of Maharashtra,

Karnataka, the Central Provinces, and Berar, while Annie's league operated throughout the rest of India.

The two leagues never merged, and although Besant claimed she had nothing against Tilak, some of his conservative convictions regarding the rights of Indian women may have kept them apart. Although Tilak had progressive beliefs when it came to the politics of India, he remained very conservative when it came to social reforms. He opposed the reforms that fought against untouchability, a practice that ostracizes minorities, in the caste system of India. He was also against raising the consent age for the marriage of girls, as he claimed it would break Hindu tradition. The consent age, according to Hindu tradition, was ten years, and the British government successfully raised it to twelve despite very strong opposition by the conservatives. However, Tilak had a great number of followers; by April 1917, his home rule league had 14,000 members.

In contrast to Tilak's league, Besant had only gathered 7,000 members by May 1917. Many of those members were followers of her Theosophical Society, and they remained inactive in Indian politics. However, Besant's strength wasn't in numbers but in the ideology she represented. While Tilak tried to make an excuse for caste differences, Besant's home league worked on setting up education centers and libraries for lower castes. She also actively worked on removing the concept of untouchability. Even though Annie Besant and Tilak had completely different views on the social status of Indians, they never publicly opposed each other since they had the same goal of promoting the self-government of India.

As both home rule leagues grew in popularity, spreading their influence through the universities of India, the British government had to react. In June 1917, Besant and her associates were arrested. However, the government didn't expect India to protest their internment so vigorously. A wave of nationwide anger toward the government's actions pushed some prominent Indians to renounce the British rule. Sir Subbier Subramania Iyar, a knight commander of the Most Eminent Order of the Indian Empire, renounced his knighthood in protest. Even those Congress members who hesitated to join the home rule movement did so at this point. Tilak called upon civilians to engage in civil disobedience until Besant and her associates were released from their imprisonment.

The unrest caused by the imprisonment of Annie Besant was effective on two fronts. She was released in September of 1917, and the new secretary of state of India, Edwin Montagu, made a historic declaration on August 20th, 1917. He stated that the new policy of employing more Indians in the government's administration was to be immediately put in effect in preparation for the development of self-governing institutions. This was a big step for both home rule leagues, but it didn't mean that India got its self-government. The British made sure to add a clause that only the British government had the power to decide when and under what conditions the self-rule would be granted.

However, the majority of members of the home rule leagues were pacified by the statement of Edwin Montagu, and they sought no further action. Instead of continuing its struggles, Annie Besant's home rule league dissolved. Even though she was promoted as the president of the Indian National Congress, her previous followers stopped attending the meetings in 1918. When the government published the intended reforms, it created another split in the Indian National Congress. Some wanted to accept what the government offered immediately, while others wanted to reject it all. Besant herself, even though she was aware of the need for further fighting, questioned the effectiveness of passive resistance. She also condemned the reforms the government offered, saying that they were an embarrassment for Britain; however, she later advocated in their favor.

Tilak was consistent in his beliefs, and he wanted to continue the fight for self-government, but he couldn't do it alone. He decided to leave for England at the end of 1918, where he sued Valentine Chirol for defamation. Tilak's absence from the political life of India during these critical months only sped up the demise of the league. Even though the league was short-lived, it did make a huge step for the self-governance of India. The members of both the Indian National Congress and the home rule leagues who remained true to their nationalistic ideology would prove to be the backbone of the movement under the leadership of Mahatma Gandhi, a man who was already famous for his efforts to improve the lives of Indians in South Africa.

Chapter 7 – Mahatma Gandhi

Photograph of Mahatma Gandhi taken in 1931

https://en.wikipedia.org/wiki/Mahatma_Gandhi#/media/File:Mahatma-Gandhi,_studio,_1931.jpg

In South Africa

An Indian lawyer, who studied in London, Mohandas Karamchand Gandhi is one of the most known people in the world. He was an Indian anti-colonialism activist and ethicist renowned for his nonviolent methods of resistance. Today, he is a symbol of pacifism and world peace, and he continues to inspire people all over the world to fight for their freedom and rights. He is well known by his honorable title Mahatma, which many confuse for his actual name. In Sanskrit, Mahatma means venerable, and he was first referred to as such during his activism in South Africa.

Indians had started their migration to South Africa during 1890, as the poverty and lack of work drove them to seek fortune beyond their homeland, mostly in other British colonies. Gandhi was invited to South Africa to represent an Indian merchant in a lawsuit. He was the first highly educated Indian to arrive in South Africa, and he chose to stay there and even bring his family with him. But young Gandhi was baffled by the racism he saw, which was a part of the everyday life of an Indian in South Africa. Gandhi was from a respected family, as his father was a dewan (state minister), and he couldn't swallow all the racial insults coming his way, either by the locals or by the white colonialists. Not even in England, where he spent three years studying, did he encounter such racism directed at him. Besides the usual verbal insults, Gandhi was denied entrance in the first-class carriage of a train, even though he had the appropriate ticket. He was instead directed to sit at the back of the train with the luggage. Another instance was at a hotel, where he had a room booked, but the management simply didn't believe him and kicked him out. He continued to experience such racist indecencies throughout his stay in South Africa.

Upon his arrival in Pretoria, where the trial was to take place, Gandhi immediately gathered his fellow Indians and offered to teach them English so they could get by in everyday life in a foreign country. He also suggested that they should oppose this oppression and organize some kind of protest against it. In addition, Gandhi voiced his displeasure through the press.

Gandhi didn't mean to settle in South Africa, and after the lawsuit was over, he prepared to go back to India. But the uneducated Indians begged him to stay at least for a month to help them organize their protests. Since they did not know the English language, they couldn't even draft the petitions, let alone understand more complicated documents. Gandhi agreed to stay for one month, but he ended up staying much longer. He arrived as a 25-year-old lawyer, and when he left, he was a 45-year-old Mahatma.

Gandhi's activism was mainly in the political sphere, as he sent numerous petitions and letters to South African legislatures, the colonial secretary in London, and to British Parliament. He was sure that the British government just needed to hear all the facts of the oppression of Indians in South Africa to make them intervene. To raise his effectiveness and unite the Indians from the worker and merchant classes, he founded the South African Indian Congress, and he also started his own newspaper, *Indian Opinion*. He was an efficient fundraiser, journalist, politician, and propagandist in one whole package. However, by 1906, Gandhi was completely convinced that the "moderate" methods he undertook were getting him nowhere.

From 1906 onward, Gandhi implemented his idea of passive resistance, which he named Satyagraha. The term itself is a combination of the Sanskrit words for "truth" and "insistence." But for Gandhi, satyagraha was more philosophical, as he explained that the truth is love and that the insistence is force. According to him, satyagraha is a "love force" that is strong enough to bring change. The core of Gandhi's philosophy was civil disobedience, although he preferred to call it "civil resistance." He preached that the best way to fight oppression was through nonviolent, passive resistance. However, this doesn't mean that the activists of satyagraha did nothing. The point was to refuse to obey the government as an alternative to violence.

For example, when the government in South Africa made it obligatory for all Indians to register and to carry their compulsory certificates of registration with them at all times, they refused to do so. When the government started prosecuting Indians for disobedience, they simply pleaded guilty and were sent to jail. However, the number of Indians in jails steadily grew, as they insisted on practicing civil disobedience. In just a few weeks, the number of jailed Indians rose to 155, and they even mockingly called it "King Edward's Hotel." Finally, the government realized that their legislation had no effect, and they had to give in. A deal was made stating that the law would be withdrawn if Indians willingly registered themself. Gandhi was the first to accept these terms, proving that his satyagraha was successful.

However, the government played a trick on the Indian activists and passed another law that restricted Indian immigration to South Africa. Gandhi and his followers realized the fight would have to continue. To support the activists and their families, Gandhi opened the Tolstoy Farm, which was a donation from his rich German friend Hermann Kallenbach, who admired Gandhi's philosophy. The farm was set to offer sustenance to the families of those Indians who were imprisoned due to civil disobedience in their fight against the government. Named after Russian author Leo Tolstoy, who greatly influenced both Gandhi and Kallenbach, the farm was one of the first ashrams, which, in this case, were similar farms opened in India during the period of Gandhi's activism in his home country.

Gandhi's nonviolent satyagraha meant several imprisonments for both him and his followers. In South African jails, they were put through hard work, starvation, and beatings, and they were constantly kept in dark cells. But the struggle continued, and the harsh environment of the prison didn't break their spirits. Once the prison conditions became public, Indian workers all over South Africa went on strike. The satyagraha forced the government to sit with its opponents at a negotiation table, and many demands of the oppressed Indians in South Africa were met. Gandhi was satisfied with the actions of his people, and he felt like he had taught them everything his philosophy had to offer. It was time for him to go back home to India and bring satyagraha there.

In India

In January 1915, Mahatma Gandhi moved back to India, where he was received with a warm welcome. His deeds in South Africa were already known to his fellow Indians back home, and although he did expect some educated colleagues to know of his actions, he was not prepared for the masses of people who came to welcome him. One of the leaders of the Indian National Congress, Gopal Krishna Gokhale, described Gandhi as a man who was made out of the stuff of which heroes and martyrs were made. For Gokhale and many Indians who admired Gandhi, that stuff was his spirit, which he used to inspire the people around him.

But for a year after his arrival, Gandhi didn't join any political activities that would bring India closer to its independence. This is because he decided to spend as much time as he needed to study the situation of India. He traveled the subcontinent to see for himself how the communities lived and what demands Indians had. Everywhere he went, he would gain a horde of followers. However, his political views were different from those of the Indian National Congress and both home rule leagues. He did not join either of them, instead deciding to go a separate way.

During 1917 and 1918, Gandhi engaged himself in local political issues, and he was active during the three important struggles of Champaran (a city in Bihar), Ahmedabad, and Kheda (cities in Gujarat). Gandhi was arrested as soon as he entered Champaran, and he offered no resistance, confusing the politicians of India. He wasn't truly a rebel by their definition, even though he came to give his support to the peasants who fought against their landowners. Thus, the local authorities were ordered to release Gandhi. He proceeded with touring the villages and taking their statements to ensure a strong case against the system. But the government decided to convey an investigation and formed a Commission of Inquiry. They even invited Gandhi to be one of the members, and he used the gathered evidence from the peasants to persuade the commission that the workers had indeed been mistreated.

After the victory in Champaran, Gandhi went to Ahmedabad, where the industrial workers were protesting the mill owners, who wanted to take away the "plague bonus" from workers' payments because the plague had passed. However, the workers needed the bonus because the living expenses had increased during the outbreak of World War I. It was a British collector, a member of the British local administration, who asked Gandhi to come and propose a compromise between the workers and the mill owners. After his investigation, Gandhi concluded that the workers needed an increase in their salaries to meet the price demands of life during the world war. He suggested workers go on strike, and during it, Gandhi encouraged them by addressing them personally every day. Because there was a danger of starvation due to going on strike, as the workers no longer received their payments, Gandhi promised he would be the first to starve, and he committed himself to fast. The pressure on the mill owners was increased by Gandhi's fasting, and they finally agreed to meet the workers' demands.

In Kheda, the peasants had the same problems as those in Champaran, but here, they were caused by the failure of crops instead of the greed of landowners. The peasants demanded the remission of the land value, but the government ignored them. Gandhi couldn't allow the people to starve, and he called upon the law, which stated that if the crop yielded less than one-fourth of the average yearly harvest, the citizens were entitled to a total remission of the land revenue. However, all his appeals and petitions to the government failed, so he called upon the peasants to practice civil disobedience. The peasants of Kheda were too exhausted, though, as they had previously been stricken with the plague and now with hunger. The government agreed to collect the revenues only from those peasants who could pay but under the condition that it did not reach the public, as it would be a blow to the government's prestige. Gandhi was compelled to agree to this condition due to the people's weak health. Even though there was no publicity given to his struggle in Kheda, Gandhi was victorious.

These three incidents were a demonstration of Gandhi's methods and their effectiveness. He also gained popularity while solving the problems of the common people around the country, and he now had the full knowledge to understand what the masses in India wanted, the masses that would be his weapon during the fight against colonial rule. The young people of India joined Gandhi's movement with every step he took. They loved how he was able to identify himself with the troubles of the common people and how he found strength and peace in pacifism.

In 1919, Gandhi already had enough followers to organize a massive protest against the British government, which planned to introduce unpopular legislation. As World War I was coming to an end, the British Raj planned to reduce the civil rights of their Indian subjects. Because of the threat that the nationalist movements in India presented, the British government wanted to extend the state of emergency that had been in place since the beginning of the war. This meant that the civil rights of a fair trial, imprisonment with defined accusations, and freedom of movement were to be restricted, if not completely taken away. These legislations were known as the Rowlatt Act, named after the president of the sedition committee who proposed them, Sidney Rowlatt.

After the protests failed, Gandhi proposed implementing his satyagraha. The younger members of the home rule leagues rushed to join Gandhi's movement, as they wanted to distance themselves from the government officials. They were the ones who reached out to their colleagues and created a huge network for spreading the propaganda of satyagraha. Gandhi's followers decided to organize a massive strike throughout the country, which would include fasting and praying.

The nationwide satyagraha was launched on April 6th, 1919, but there was some confusion with the date in some parts of India, as Delhi held their strike on March 30th. There was also a lot of violence on the streets of the city, which was against everything that satyagraha stood for. Violence spread through other cities, and it culminated in Punjab, where the people had suffered the most during the war. They had been hit by diseases, hunger, and excessive recruitment for the war. Gandhi tried to reach Punjab and pacify its people, but the British government deported him to Bombay. Since Bombay was in flames too, he decided to stay there and help calm down the situation.

In the city of Amritsar in Punjab, the situation escalated to include some very tragic events. The locals started attacking British citizens, including women and children. Because of the violence, the government decided to call in the army and hand the city to General Reginald Dyer, who immediately took action by prohibiting public meetings. However, April 13th was the festival of Vaisakhi, which both Sikhs and Hindus celebrate. A large crowd of people gathered to observe the holiday, and even the peasants from neighboring villages flocked to the city. This was in direct defiance to General Dyer's orders, and he ordered his troops to start shooting at the unarmed crowd for a full ten minutes. He didn't even warn the people, who were trapped, as the city was walled, offering no place to run or hide. The official count was 379 dead, but unofficial numbers go much higher. Over 1,000 people were injured. The youngest victim of what became known as the Amritsar massacre was a six-week-old baby. The Indian National Congress decided to investigate the casualties for themselves, as the numbers offered by the British government did not match the number of fires shot and the number of attendants, which was roughly around 20,000. They concluded that around 1,000 people were killed, with 500 dying later due to the wounds they had received.

Even though the massacre stunned the whole nation, the situation in Punjab only got worse. Martial law was in effect, and so, the people were put through various indignities, such as being forced to crawl on their bellies and to kiss the boots of the Europeans. The brutality that took place in Punjab made Gandhi and his followers withdraw their strike. However, Mahatma Gandhi didn't lose faith in his people. Only a year later, he started another nationwide strike, and the Amritsar massacre was just one of the reasons for its launch.

The Non-cooperation Movement

The Amritsar massacre and the increased violence in Punjab horrified Gandhi, and he made a promise that if India united in the efforts of nonviolent protests, the Swaraj (self-government) would come in a year. He didn't believe anymore in the good intentions of the British, as no government could commit such a crime on its subjects and be willing to make changes for the better. But Gandhi was the only one who was revolted by the actions of the British government. The First World War had just ended, and the people realized that the British had made many post-war promises that they had no intention of keeping. The people were still as hungry as they were during the war, they still died of preventable diseases due to the poor healthcare system, and they were still treated as uncivilized subhumans by the Europeans.

But one of the promises that Britain didn't keep after the war brought about the wrath of the Muslims, who finally joined Gandhi's movement. The British had promised that after the world war, the Ottoman Caliphate would be restored. The Ottoman rulers were considered to be the leaders of the Sunni faith and politics. The Treaty of Sèvres, signed a few years after the end of the First World War in 1920, partitioned the Ottoman Empire and the Sunni Caliphate, which only angered the Muslims in India. In protest of the Treaty of Sèvres, the Indian Muslims organized a movement of their own, known as the Khilafat movement. Gandhi was sympathetic to their cause and invited them to join other Indians in protest against the British Raj, which the members of the Khilafat movement gladly accepted.

Even the Indian National Congress agreed that not much could be achieved through constitutional means, and many members joined Gandhi's non-cooperation movement. They called upon their colleagues to not comply with the legislative matters of the British government and to withdraw from the upcoming parliamentary elections. Even the voters refused to vote. Some of the Congress members didn't agree with the decision to boycott elections, but under the pressure of their party, they complied and withdrew. Annie Besant supported India's fight for self-governance, but she didn't agree with the socialist ideas. She left the Congress and continued to advocate India's independence on her own, through various campaigns both in India and in England.

Formally, the movement was launched on August 1st with a nationwide protest (hartal) taking place. On the same day, in the early morning hours, Bal Gangadhar Tilak died, and many people began fasting and praying as they mourned his passing. Some scholars place September 4th as the official date when the non-cooperation movement was launched, as that is the day the Indian National Congress joined the movement. By December, the members of the Congress decided to surrender all of their honors and titles and boycott British schools, laws, clothing, and taxes.

Congress worked on opening Indian schools, and they also founded Panchayats, which are local self-governments that have the authority to settle disputes. Members of Congress also encouraged the domestic production of textiles and asked all Hindus and Muslims to live in unity and give up the practice of untouchability. The nationwide movement for nonviolent disobedience was set in place, and even the extreme revolutionary terrorists from Bengal joined the movement and stopped their guerilla attacks.

During 1921, Gandhi and the leaders of the Khilafat movement went on a national tour of the country, organizing many gatherings with various politicians and addressing the common people personally. In the first month alone, their movement influenced around 90,000 students to leave British schools and enroll in newly opened national schools. Lawyers even refused to enter courts and follow the British laws, sacrificing their lucrative careers. This served to inspire more people to join the movement.

However, it seems that the boycott of British textiles and clothing had the most effect. Volunteers were organized, and they went from house to house to collect all foreign clothing, which they burned in a bonfire. They didn't burn only the clothes, as the boycott expanded to include all foreign products. Government revenues that were brought about by selling foreign products in India declined so much that the British were forced to implement new propaganda that would persuade Indians that foreign goods were beneficial to them. However, this propaganda had little effect.

Mohammed Ali Jauhar, one of the leaders of the Khilafat movement, was arrested after he made a statement that it went against Islam to serve in the British Army and that all Muslim sepoys should immediately leave. Gandhi supported Jauhar, and he issued a manifesto in which he repeated Jauhar's words. Gandhi also made a call to all Indian soldiers of any religion to sever their ties with the British Army. The Indian National Congress adopted the same resolution and continued to spread propaganda among the Indian soldiers. The British government was essentially powerless, and they couldn't do anything to persuade the Indians to join their army. It was the first victory of the non-cooperation movement, as the British government had to capitulate and take the blow to its prestige. The second blow occurred when the prince of Wales, Edward VIII, visited India. He landed in Bombay and planned a public tour of the city. However, all the streets were empty on that day, and all the windows had their shutters down.

Despite the successes that the non-cooperation movement achieved with its use of nonviolence, Indians around the country were somehow inspired to turn to aggression. At first, the violent acts were small and didn't cause much trouble with the local authorities, but Gandhi was worried that the movement would turn away from his pacifist views. The British government didn't take any actions against the movement in the beginning, thinking it would quickly pass. But when the Khilafat leaders started openly talking about violence during their meetings, the government decided to act. They started arresting all the leaders of both the Khilafat movement and Congress. Soon, the leaders of the non-cooperation movement were arrested as well, and only Gandhi was still free. The government proclaimed any large gatherings of people to be illegal, and they started raids on the offices and homes of the movement's officials. In total, 30,000 people were arrested around the country.

Gandhi had no other choice but to call for nationwide civil disobedience once again, as his pleas to Rufus Isaacs, the viceroy of India, to release the political prisoners were ignored. However, on February 5th, 1922, the civil disobedience turned into another massacre, this time in the small town of Chauri Chaura in the United Provinces. There, the protesters attacked the policemen who tried to stop their picketing of a liquor shop. A conflict between the protesters and police broke out, which led to a police station being set on fire with 22 officers still inside. Gandhi was revolted by this incident, and he called off the movement. He even persuaded the Indian National Congress to ratify his decision. Single-handedly, Gandhi had ended the non-cooperation movement on February 15th, 1922. He was arrested on March 10th and sentenced to six years of imprisonment on the charges of sedition.

Gandhi was released from prison due to his declining health on February 5th, 1924. The new nationalist political party, the Swaraj Party, had already been constructed out of the remnants of the Indian National Congress and the non-cooperation movement. But they had a different agenda than the nonviolent approach of their predecessors. Their plan was not to boycott the British government but to enter and bring it down from within. Gandhi didn't agree with the new methods the nationalists had in mind, but he also didn't stand in their way. The years between 1922 and 1927 were years of separate activism movements, each working for its own agenda. However, no results were achieved, and the atmosphere of apathy and frustration prevailed in all the nationalist organizations. It seemed as if they all needed a break to rest and recoup.

However, this doesn't mean that the whole of India stopped its resistance to British rule. There were many movements on the rise that tell their own stories, but they all ultimately failed. Some of them won small victories but led India no closer to its independence. The revolutionary terrorists were also on the rise with guerilla warfare in the Bengal province. But government actions decimated their numbers, and with the death of their leader in 1931, the revolutionary movement came to an end. The revolutionaries didn't have a clear political plan, and because of that, they were unable to move the masses and gain their trust. However, their willingness to sacrifice themselves did touch the Indian nation and inspired them to take action once more. Indians were reminded of their nationalism and patriotic sentiment, and they were ready to take the fight into their own hands.

The Salt March

The Salt March led by Gandhi

The Swaraj Party fell apart after the death of its leader, Chittaranjan Das, in 1925. The Indian National Congress reorganized itself, and they rose in protest when the British government decided to form a commission that would look at the Indian constitution and make changes. The problem was that the commission was composed only of Europeans. Since Sir John Simon was at its head, it is remembered as the Simon Commission. The Indians were outraged that they were not even considered for such a task, and the organized protests only grew in power after the freedom fighter Lala Lajpat Rai died due to severe beatings by the police.

As a response to the Simon Commission, the Indian National Congress appointed its own members to form a similar commission and propose their changes to the British government. The idea was to give India self-government within the British Empire, but the British decided to ignore both the Congress and their commission. As a result, the Congress only grew in its determination, and once the negotiations with the government failed, they brought up the declaration of India's independence, known as Purna Swaraj (complete self-rule).

On December 31st, 1929, the new president of the Congress, Jawaharlal Nehru, hoisted the flag of India in Lahore. They proclaimed January 26th as the Independence Day of India, and the Indian flag was displayed throughout the whole subcontinent. In February 1930, the Congress asked Gandhi to launch a civil disobedience movement, giving him all the power to decide the time, place, and the political program of it. Gandhi chose the British government's salt laws as the first issue that the movement would address.

The Salt Act of 1882 instituted a British monopoly on salt gathering, production, and distribution. The taxes they imposed were too high for the common people of India to pay, and according to the Salt Act, any intent to acquire salt by any other means was a criminal offense. Even though Indians could have produced their own salt easily by evaporating seawater, they were prohibited from doing so.

The Indian National Congress thought the salt laws were not a good starting point, as they couldn't see how a protest against it would affect the government. Indeed, even the viceroy of India, Lord Edward Irwin, thought the announced protests wouldn't give him too much trouble, and the British government openly laughed at Gandhi's idea. However, Gandhi had a good reason for choosing the salt laws. Salt was a commodity everyone needed, for without it, life would be impossible. Thus, the protest against the British monopoly on salt was a thing that concerned all the people of India, every caste, every religion, and every individual, no matter their age. Gandhi knew that if he organized a political protest with ideas such as civil rights, the common people wouldn't respond as readily, as politics were an abstract idea for the majority of them.

Gandhi's belief of nonviolence and his philosophy of satyagraha led him to choose a march as his first means of civil disobedience in his fight against the salt laws. He notified the viceroy of India about the details of his march, and the first reports of Gandhi's intentions to defy the salt laws were published in the press on February 5th, 1930. Gandhi invited media from all over the world to announce the march, and he often held vigorous speeches insisting on the importance of nonviolence and civil disobedience. On March 2nd, he wrote again to Viceroy Lord Irwin, asking him to meet his demands of, among others, land revenue assessments, cutting military spending, and the abolishment of the salt tax. He even promised he would withdraw from the announced march, but the viceroy ignored him.

Gandhi's march began on March 12th in Sabarmati Ashram, the suburbs of Ahmedabad. Eighty of his followers from Sabarmati Ashram designated as his marching companions, and they were chosen because they were representatives of various castes and were trained in Gandhi's satyagraha. The route of the march was well planned, and the procession was to visit 48 villages that had been specifically chosen because of their recruitment potential. The Salt March lasted for 24 days and ended in Dandi, Gujarat. On his way, Gandhi walked 240 miles (390 kilometers), stopping in each village to hold a speech to inspire more people to join him. Soon, he was followed by thousands of people, all wearing white clothes, which was why the march was named "White Flowing River." Gandhi never stopped giving interviews for the media that followed him, and he even wrote his own articles and news reports. The *New York Times* wrote about Gandhi's progression daily, while many foreign news companies chose to shoot newsreel footage.

The Salt March ended on April 6th when the procession reached the seashore. There, Gandhi raised a hunk of salty mud from the ground and boiled it in seawater, producing illegal salt. With this act, he officially started the civil disobedience movement. He instructed his followers to produce illegal salt wherever it was possible, and this movement is often seen as the start of the fall of the British rule in India. Chakravarti Rajagopalachari organized his own salt march on the east coast. At the end of his route, he was arrested by the British authorities.

Gandhi anticipated the police to arrest him as well, but it didn't happen. The British government was confused by the peaceful disobedience and didn't know how to react. They preferred an enemy who fought back and had no idea how to fight nonviolence. A month later, Mahatma Gandhi was arrested and accused of instigating protests. But the government reaction came too late, as the civil disobedience movement had already spread throughout the country. Peasants refused to pay taxes, illegal salt was being produced and sold everywhere, and a new wave of boycotts of foreign products started.

Unfortunately, in some provinces, violence erupted. However, unlike during the non-cooperation movement, Gandhi did not withdraw. He condemned the violence and advocated for its end, but he was committed to the movement. The violence culminated in Peshawar, where British soldiers fired on a crowd that was peacefully protesting the arrest of their leader, Abdul Ghaffar Khan. Around 200 unarmed Indian protesters lost their lives.

Gandhi succeeded in his attempt to make the salt laws into a cause that would shake the whole nation. After his arrest, people became ever more innovative in coming up with different forms of civil disobedience. Boycotts of everything foreign began anew, and this time, women were leaders. Never before did India see the raw strength of their women. Even those who covered their faces with veils in the practice of purdah (the seclusion of females in Muslim and Hindu cultures) stood strong in front of the various storefronts that sold British goods, successfully changing the minds of both buyers and shopkeepers. Gandhi admired women, and his philosophy promoted more freedom for females; however, it should be noted that he was a conservative in a gentler form. He believed that a woman should only get an education that would help her play the traditional role of a mother and wife.

While Indians nonviolently and effectively protested all over the subcontinent, the British government sought ways to achieve some kind of compromise with the people. Gandhi was invited to a Round Table Conference in London in 1930, where the talks about the Indian constitution were to happen. But once he was there, he was told not to expect to talk about the independence of India. Even though the conference was ultimately unsuccessful for the Indians, the conference was still the first event in history in which the British and Indians sat at a table as equals. When Gandhi returned home, the British released all of the political prisoners of the civil disobedience movement. On March 5th, 1931, Gandhi and Viceroy Lord Irwin signed a truce known as the Gandhi-Irwin Pact. The British monopoly on salt production and trade was lifted, meaning Indians could legally make, sell, and buy their own salt again.

The Salt March remains one of the most important moments in human history. It is estimated that around 90,000 Indians were arrested during the protests that followed. The Salt March also inspired the fight against oppressive regimes all around the world. In the US, Martin Luther King Jr. admired Gandhi's idea of uniting the people around a common cause. In South Africa, Nelson Mandela used some of the satyagraha methods while overthrowing the apartheid system. People of all nations around the world still use peaceful, nonviolent protests to voice their disagreements with the acts of their governments.

Chapter 8 – World War II, the "Quit India" Movement, and Independence

Indian soldiers in Burma

https://en.wikipedia.org/wiki/India_in_World_War_II#/media/
File:INDIAN_TROOPS_IN_BURMA,_1944.jpg

World War II is generally thought to have started when the German forces invaded Poland on September 1ˢᵗ, 1939. The first to respond were France and the United Kingdom. Although the first battles were fought on European soil, India, under the rule of the British Raj, joined the war just a few days after its start. The Indian viceroy at the time, Lord Linlithgow, didn't even bother to consult with the leading Indian politicians or listen to public opinion. Instead, he declared that India would fight on the side of Britain, undermining the previous efforts of India to gain its independence. The faraway war took over 2.5 million soldiers from India, who defended the territories of other British colonies, such as Singapore and Hong Kong. The Indian soldiers also fought in the territories of Europe and Africa—they went pretty much wherever the Allies needed them. During the war, the British government led India into debt by taking a couple of billion pounds from India, which was needed to finance the war. The measures the British implemented within India were so oppressive that they directly caused the Bengal famine of 1943, which they declined to implement a relief program for. In Burma and British Malaya, the European soldiers and inhabitants of these colonies were safely evacuated, leaving the locals and Indian soldiers to fend for themselves.

The biggest political party of India at the time was the Indian National Congress, whose leadership was entrusted to Mahatma Gandhi, Maulana Abul Kalam Azad, and Vallabhbhai Patel (more commonly known as Sardar Patel). They agreed to decline help to the British government during the Second World War, even though they personally condemned the actions of Nazi Germany and Adolf Hitler. They promised their help only under the condition that India gained its independence. The British were not expecting the Indian National Congress to react this way, and they were baffled by their decision. However, India wasn't united in their decision to decline help to the British. The All-India Muslim League and some of the smaller political parties actually gave their support to the British government. But the Congress demanded that Britain transfer all its governmental power to them. Unable to comply, the two found themselves in a stalemate. The provincial governments failed due to the mass resignation of the members of the Congress, and the probability of a nationwide revolt became very real.

The British government continued its efforts to persuade the Indian National Congress to find common ground. But all the negotiations failed, and time was running out, as Japan declared war on the Dutch and Britain in December 1941. The British defeat in Singapore, which Japan took over in February 1942, was a great blow to the British government's confidence. Some Indian politicians saw Japan's entry into the war as an opportunity. Subhas Chandra Bose, for instance, thought he could give his support to Japan and Germany and use their help to get rid of British rule. He founded the Indian National Army with Japan, which fought against the Allies. Afraid of the consequences of Bose's actions and after the loss of Singapore, the British government was forced to react.

British Prime Minister Winston Churchill sent Sir Stafford Cripps to negotiate for the pan-Indian support for the war in April 1942. For this, Cripps needed to get the Congress leaders and the All-India Muslim League to agree. Cripps belonged to a political party that supported Indian self-governance, and he did bring this promise to the negotiating table. However, the All-India Muslim League wanted a separate Muslim state after the war. It was impossible to satisfy both the Indian National Congress and the All-India Muslim League. On top of that, Churchill wasn't satisfied with Cripps's proposal that India should gain the status of a dominion (semi-independent states). The negotiations quickly fell apart, and Sir Stafford Cripps had no other choice but to proclaim his mission as a failure.

After unsuccessful negotiations with the British diplomat, it became clear to the Indian National Congress that Britain had no intention of letting India go. India's unwilling partnership in World War II was to be continued, which went against everything that Gandhi's satyagraha stood for. Even though he didn't want to do anything that would obstruct the British efforts against Nazi Germany, Gandhi finally realized that it was impossible to stay silent and let the Allies and the Axis Powers divide India for their own use. He spent the spring drafting a resolution for the Congress that called for Britain's departure from India and the adoption of nonviolent methods in their efforts against Japan. By August 1942, the Indian National Congress adopted this resolution, and the movement became known as "Quit India," after the slogan that followed it, "Bharat Chhodo."

Mahatma Gandhi made a very powerful speech on the eve of the creation of the "Quit India" movement. He called for passive resistance and made a comparison with the French and Russian revolutions, saying that they failed in their achievement of democratic ideals because they were fought with weapons. India was to gain its freedom by nonviolence. However, the slogan he gave to the people was "do or die," which he interpreted as the will to persist in their efforts until India finally became independent. In his words, Indians would rather die than endure everlasting slavery to the British Raj.

Instructing his people in nonviolent disobedience, Gandhi asked them to wait for the official launch of the movement, as he wanted to give one more chance to the viceroy of India to accept their terms. But the government was in no mood to negotiate again. Instead, on August 9th, they launched a series of arrests targeted at the leaders and members of the Indian National Congress, as well as anyone who opposed their rule. Around 90,000 people were arrested in a single swipe, as the British were anticipating some kind of revolution. However, these government actions backfired, as they did not foresee the aggressive reactions of the Indians to these arrests. The leaderless people managed to gather and oppose local authorities in response to the arrests. Bombay, Ahmedabad, and Pune were the first to rise, and only a few days later, Delhi, Allahabad, Kanpur, and Patna, among others, joined in. The people openly defied the British laws and organized hartals, mass protests, in cities and towns around India.

To stop the spreading unrest, the British government banned all press from reporting about the "Quit India" movement. However, only the *National Herald* and *Harijan* ceased writing about the struggle during its duration. Gandhi himself was arrested, but he made sure to leave behind written instructions on how to peacefully disobey the British rule. He proposed that students should leave their studies, that workers should strike, and that villagers should stop paying taxes. He also invited the people of the princely states to join the rest of India and for the princes to abandon their support of the British government. However, it was the common people who proved to be the most imaginative in disobeying the laws. The symbols of the governmental rule, such as railway stations, police stations, and courts, were constantly under attack. Indians would hoist the national flag of India on these buildings to demonstrate their anger. The villagers would also gather in groups of hundreds and dismantle the nearby railroads. Bridges were blown up, and telephone and telegraph lines were cut. All of these were the symbols of British rule, and the people felt the need to get rid of them.

Students quit their studies as Gandhi proposed and devoted their time to volunteering in the movement by spreading the news all around India. They printed illegal newspapers, which they would then distribute to nearby villages, calling on the peasants to join the uprising. Students also acted as couriers for the underground network of rebels that organized worker strikes all over the subcontinent. It was the students who called for the burning of police and railway stations and who hijacked the local trains to paint them in the national colors of India. The movement was the strongest in Bihar, where for two weeks, no government authority existed, as the officials had fled from the angry populace. Unfortunately, the people of India indulged in violence, and some European civilians were attacked. As Gandhi later explained, Indians couldn't differentiate between the British Empire and the British people. To them, they were one and the same. Fighting one meant fighting the other, and a number of British who lived in India died.

The British government did not sit idle, and the suppression of the uprisings was installed almost immediately. The police freely shot at the unarmed crowds of demonstrators, and the government also approved of low-flying aircraft machine-gunning civilians. The hostages the British captured were taken from their villages, and collective fines were imposed on disobedient settlements. In some cases, the government burned whole villages down if they suspected they were hiding resistance fighters. Even though martial law wasn't proclaimed, the army was free to do whatever they wanted. The soldiers would beat citizens, often torturing and killing them whenever they had the opportunity. The mass gatherings and violence against the government symbols stopped after six weeks of brutal repression. However, the movement continued to operate underground.

The British government called on Gandhi to condemn the violence of the people, but he refused to do so, saying that the fault lay with the British rule, not the people. Furthermore, on February 10th, 1943, he started a fast while in jail as a reply to the government's efforts to belittle him. The news of Gandhi's fast quickly spread around the country, and once more, the subcontinent turned to protests, strikes, and demonstrations. Prisoners of various jails throughout India sympathized with the leader of the "Quit India" movement and went on hunger strikes of their own.

The people of India gathered in masses to demand Gandhi's release from prison. Some even traveled to openly protest in front of Aga Khan Palace, where Gandhi was detained. Soon enough, word spread around the world, and people from various countries bombarded the British government of India with letters and telegraphs demanding his release. The press joined the call, and newspapers such as the *Chicago Sun*, *News Chronicle*, and *Manchester Guardian* openly challenged the British Raj. Various local and world organizations followed suit, including the British Communist Party, the Women's International League, the Australian Council of Trade Unions, and even the United States government.

However, the British government, under the leadership of Prime Minister Churchill, was unmoved. A feeling that the "Quit India" movement had failed spread throughout the nation. As a result, morale slowly declined as it seemed that the people had given up.

Gandhi was to remain in prison until May 6th, 1944, when he was finally released because of his weakened health. With his release, the struggle for India's independence continued with renewed vigor. Gandhi mostly focused on uniting the Indian people under the same cause. Although there would always be supporters of the British Raj among the locals, their numbers were getting smaller by each passing month. By 1945, the national support for India's independence outgrew the area ruled by the British Raj. The slow repatriation of foreign soldiers who had served in India during World War II led to several mutinies in the army. Even though these mutinies were quickly suppressed, it became clear to all parties where the support of the whole nation was. The same year, Clement Attlee, who had argued for India's independence since the beginning of his political career, became Britain's new prime minister. He organized the Cabinet Mission, whose sole purpose was to peacefully transfer governmental powers to India.

However, the problem of Pakistan remained. Muslims wanted their own state, while the Indian National Congress advocated for a united Indian state. The British believed that an election would settle this issue, and it was held in December 1945. The Indian National Congress won 59 governmental seats, while the All-India Muslim League won 30. The Europeans got eight, and the rest was divided between the smaller parties. However, Muslims continued to demand separation. To appease them, the Cabinet Mission came up with the plan in which India would remain united but with internal state groupings, which would allow Muslims to have autonomy within the provinces where they ruled. The All-India Muslim League agreed to these terms, but the Indian National Congress rejected them, fearing it would weaken their hold on the whole subcontinent. Angered, the

Muslims started protesting and even attacked Hindus in Calcutta. The Hindus answered the violence with more violence, and what is known as the "Great Calcutta Killing of 1946" occurred, where around 4,000 people lost their lives.

When the British prime minister appointed Lord Louis Mountbatten as the last viceroy of India with the task of overseeing the transition of power to an independent India by 1948, the leaders of the Indian National Congress pursued ways to speed up the process. They accepted the partition that the Muslims wanted, and they also sought ways to stop the violence that had spread from Calcutta to other regions of India. The fear of a Hindu-Muslim civil war led other Congress leaders to accept the partition as well.

Gandhi, however, opposed the partition, as he felt it went against all of his beliefs of a united India that would accept different religions. In spite of this, other leaders agreed that Pakistan already existed within India and that to ignore it would only lead to even more violence. The Partition Council was formed in 1947, and the division of public assets began. The areas and territories that were predominantly populated by Hindus and Sikhs were to belong to the new India, while predominantly Muslim areas were to become Pakistan. The provinces of Punjab and Bengal had to be divided between the two states, as they had mixed populations of both Muslims and Hindus. However, this didn't go peacefully. Violence erupted in the areas that were to be the new borders, a kind of violence that none of the politicians foresaw. Exhausted by World War II and unable to deal with the civil war that was rising in India, Britain decided to speed up the independence of the nation. August 14th, 1947, is the official date of the birth of the Dominion of Pakistan, with its dominion status ending in 1956. On August 15th, 1947, India gained its independence. The British Raj was no more.

Conclusion

The departure of Britain left India in a state of civil war. Violence emerging on the borderlines of the two new states resulted in many Hindu and Muslim refugees who needed new homes. Gandhi continued to work for the good of his people and eventually came to terms with the partition. Unfortunately, the killings happened on both sides of the new border, and the death rate is calculated to be between 200,000 and 2 million. The resettlement of the refugees lasted until 1951, and the city of Delhi took in most of them. With that move, its population spiked, and it remains one of the most populated cities in the world. Hindus continue to migrate to India to this day due to the religious persecutions they are exposed to in Pakistan. The partition of the Indian subcontinent is still one of the most controversial events of the 20th century.

Mahatma Gandhi was assassinated on January 30th, 1948, and his killer, Nathuram Godse, claims he did it because he blamed Gandhi for all the violence that happened due to the partition. He belonged to the extremist Hindu Mahasabha party, which believed that Gandhi was too compliant with the Muslims.

Once India became an independent state, the decision was made to keep British political ideologies intact, such as democracy, the rule of law, and, to some extent, the equality of people. Some of the institutions founded by the British Raj and the ideas behind them remain active to this day. The universities and colleges, the stock exchange, and civil services still function, for the most part, as they did before.

But what of all the British people who had built their lives in India? Where are they now? Most of them left, but some decided to stay. Many had Indian wives and children, and as such, they couldn't simply leave. Some continued to work for the Indian government, while some chose to retire and spend their days with their families. They had to adjust to the new situation the best they could. However, most of them had to leave anyways. This was not because they were expelled out of the country but because their duties called them back home. The cultural transition these individuals had to undergo left a deep scar on their personalities. Life in India was very different than that in Britain. Many of them also left behind their Indian lovers, wives, and children to return to British wives and legitimate offspring. Some returned with opium addictions, while others couldn't cope with the depression that followed, a depression caused by the abandonment of the only lives they knew.

As the British Raj left its mark on the Indian subcontinent, the people who returned to Britain were permanently marked by the lives they had once led in India.

References

Bengal Famine Code. National Institute of Public Administration, Dacca University Campus, 1967.

Beveridge, Henry. *A Comprehensive History of India, Civil, Military and Social, from the First Landing of the English, to the Suppression of the Sepoy Revolt; Including an Outline of the Early History of Hindoostan.* Blackie and Son, 1880.

Foster, William, and Patrick J. N. Tuck. *The East India Company: 1600-1858.* Routledge, 1998.

Gandhi, and Gopal Gandhi. *The Oxford India Gandhi: Essential Writings.* Oxford University Press, 2008.

Golant, William. *The British Raj.* 1988.

Sharma, Sanjay. *Famine, Philanthropy and the Colonial State: North India in the Early Nineteenth Century.* Oxford University Press, 2001.

Shastitko Petr Mikhailovich., and Savitri Shahani. *Nana Sahib: An Account of the People's Revolt in India, 1857-1859.* Shubhada Saraswat Publications, 1980.

Here's another book by Captivating History that you might be interested in

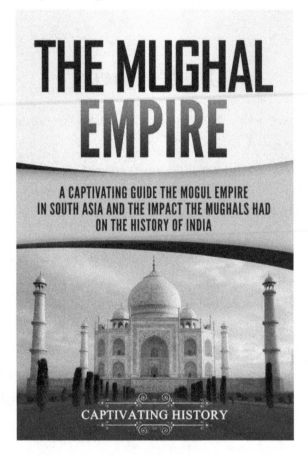

CPSIA information can be obtained
at www.ICGtesting.com
Printed in the USA
LVHW090739210721
693201LV00013BA/2051

9 781647 488345